JUL 2009 29.25
W9-AZS-469

WITHDRAWN

PASSPORT TO THE PAST

THE AZTEC AND MAYAN WORLDS

Fiona Macdonald

rosen publishing's
rosen central
New York

HIGHLAND PARK PUBLIC LIBRARY
494 LAUREL AVE.
HIGHLAND PARK, IL 60035-2690
847-432-0216

J
972.01
AZ99m

This edition published in 2009 by:

The Rosen Publishing Group, Inc.
29 East 21st Street
New York, NY 10010

Additional end matter copyright © 2009 by The Rosen Publishing Group, Inc.

All rights reserved. No part of this book may be reproduced in any form without permission in writing from the publisher, except by a reviewer.

Library of Congress Cataloging-in-Publication

Macdonald, Fiona, 1958–
The Aztec and Mayan worlds / Fiona Macdonald.
p. cm.—(Passport to the past)
Includes bibliographical references and index.
ISBN-13: 978-1-4358-5170-2 (library binding)
1. Aztecs—Social life and customs. 2. Mayas—Social life and customs. I. Title.
F1219.73.M325 2009
972'.01—dc22

2008036733

Manufactured in the United States of America

Metric Conversion Chart
1 inch = 2.54 centimeters; 25.4 millimeters
1 foot = 30.48 centimeters
1 yard = .914 meters
1 square foot = .093 square meters
1 mile = 1.609 kilometers
1 ton = .907 metric tons
1 pound = 454 grams

1 cup = 250 milliliters
1 quart = .946 liters
1 ounce = 28 grams
1 fluid ounce = 30 milliliters
1 teaspoon = 5 milliliters
1 tablespoon = 15 milliliters

A note about the crafts and recipes in this book: Adult supervision is recommended for projects involving knives or blades, a stove, or an oven.

Copyright in design, text and images © 1998, 2007 Anness Publishing Limited, U.K. Previously published as *Step Into the Aztec and Maya Worlds*.

PICTURE CREDITS
b=bottom, t=top, c=center, l=left, r=right
The Bridgeman Art Library: 9tl, 24bl, 29tr, 45bl; GDR Barnett Images: 20tl; 21bl, 42bl; The British Museum: front cover; The Bodleian Library: 13cl, 14b, 15br, 17c; Bruce Coleman: 27c; Dagli Orti 59tl; James Davis: 1, 8br, 18tl, 39bl, 50c, 52tl, 59br; C M Dixon: 10tl, 14tl, 16r, 27bl; E T Archive: 9br, 10br, 11bl, 11tr, 13tl, 15bl, 21tr, 22tl, 23br, 24tl, 25br, 26tl, 27tr, 28c, 30, 31, 32b, 33, 35tl, 36bl, 39r, 41tl, 41tr, 41bl, 42tl, 47tl, 51l, 51tr, 52c, 53c, 54, 55, 56cr, 56tl, 58t, 60br ; Mary Evans Picture Library: 22br, 39tl, 60tl; Werner Forman Archive: 4tl, 15tr, 28tl, 36tl, 55tl; Michael Holford: 5c, 11br, 12br, 34tl, 43tr, 50tl, 51r, 61; Hutchison: 37c; NHPA: 27c; Planet Earth Pictures: 25c; Scala/Art Resource NY: 16tl; South American Photo Library 4br, 5tl, 8tl, 9tl, 12tl, 13tr, 17tl, 18tr, 19tr, 20b, 22bl, 23bl, 24br, 26bl, 30bl, 33br, 35bl, 37, 43br, 44tl, 46c, 48c, 53b, 57tl, 57c, 58b, 61; Visual Arts Library: 10br, 19t, 19b, 27tl, 29tc, 29tl, 32tl, 33tl, 38cr, 40c, 40tl, 43bl, 45t, 46tl, 47tr, 55tl, 56tr, 56cl, 59tr, 60bl; Zefa: 43tr.

CONTENTS

Great Civilizations..... 4
Between North and South..... 6
Famous People..... 8
The Order of Things..... 10
The Court, Government, and Laws..... 12
Family Life..... 14
In the Home..... 16
Villages and Towns..... 18
Buildings and Houses..... 20
City in the Lake..... 22
Farming..... 24
Hunting and Gathering..... 26
Food and Drink..... 28
Keeping Healthy and Clean..... 30
Clothes, Hairstyles, and Jewelry.... 32
Craftworkers..... 34

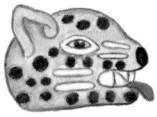

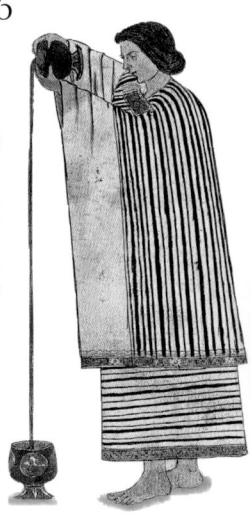

Merchants and Markets..... 36
Travel and Transport..... 38
Warriors and Weapons..... 40
Rival City-States..... 42
Aztec Conquests..... 44
Scholars and Scribes..... 46
Time, Sun, and Stars..... 48
Gods and Goddesses..... 50
Temples and Sacrifices..... 52
Time for Celebration..... 54
Sports and Games..... 56
Myths, Legends, and Omens..... 58
The Coming of the Spanish..... 60
Glossary..... 62
For More Information..... 62
For Further Reading..... 63
Index..... 63

Olmec Power
This giant stone head was carved by the Olmecs, the earliest of many great civilizations that flourished in Mesoamerica. Like the Maya and Aztecs, the Olmecs were skilled stone workers and built great cities.

Great Civilizations

The Aztecs lived in Mesoamerica—the region where North and South America meet. It includes the countries of Mexico, Guatemala, Honduras, El Salvador, and Belize. During the past 3,000 years, Mesoamerica has been home to many great civilizations, including the Olmecs, the Maya, the Toltecs, and the Aztecs. The Aztecs were the last of these to arrive, coming from the north around 1200 CE. In about 1420, they began to build a mighty empire. But in 1521, they were themselves conquered by Spanish soldiers, who had come to the Americas in search of gold. Over the next hundred years, the rest of Mesoamerica also fell to the Spaniards.

Even so, the descendants of the Aztec cultures still live in the area today. Many ancient Mesoamerican words, customs, and beliefs survive, as do beautiful hand-painted books, mysterious ruins, and amazing treasures.

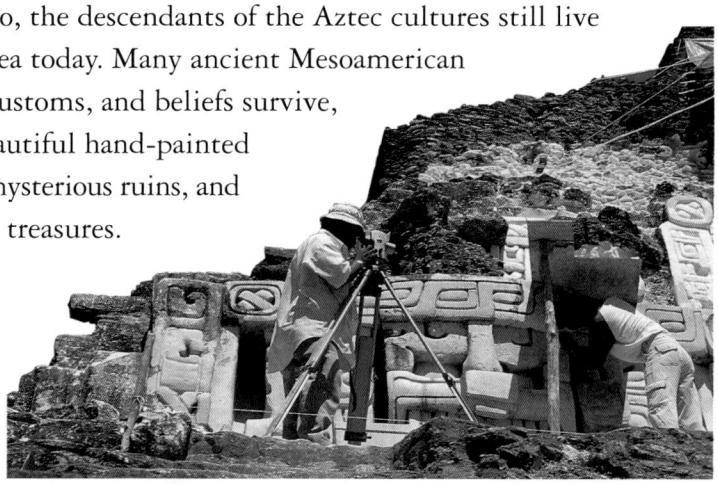

Uncovering the Past
This temple is in Belize. Remains of such great buildings give archaeologists important clues about the people who built them.

Timeline 5000 BCE–800 CE

Many civilizations were powerful in Mesoamerica at different times. The Maya were most successful between 600–900 CE. The Aztecs were at the height of their power from 1428–1520 CE.

5000 BCE The Maya settle along the Pacific and Caribbean coasts of Mesoamerica.

2000 BCE People begin to farm in Guatemala, Belize, southeast Mexico.

Olmec figure

2000 BCE The beginning of the period known as the Preclassic era.

1200 BCE Olmec people are powerful in Mesoamerica. They remain an important power until 400 BCE.

1000 BCE Mayan craftworkers begin to copy Olmec pottery and jade carvings.

900 BCE Mayan farmers design and use irrigation systems.

600 BCE The Zapotec civilization begins to flourish at Monte Alban.

Maya codex

300 BCE The Mayan population starts to grow rapidly. Cities are built.

292 BCE The first-known Mayan writing is produced.

150 BCE–500 CE The people living in the city of Teotihuacan grow powerful.

250 CE The beginning of the greatest period of Mayan power, known as the Classic Maya era. This lasts until 900 CE.

mask from Teotihuacan

5000 BCE 2000 BCE 300 BCE 500 CE

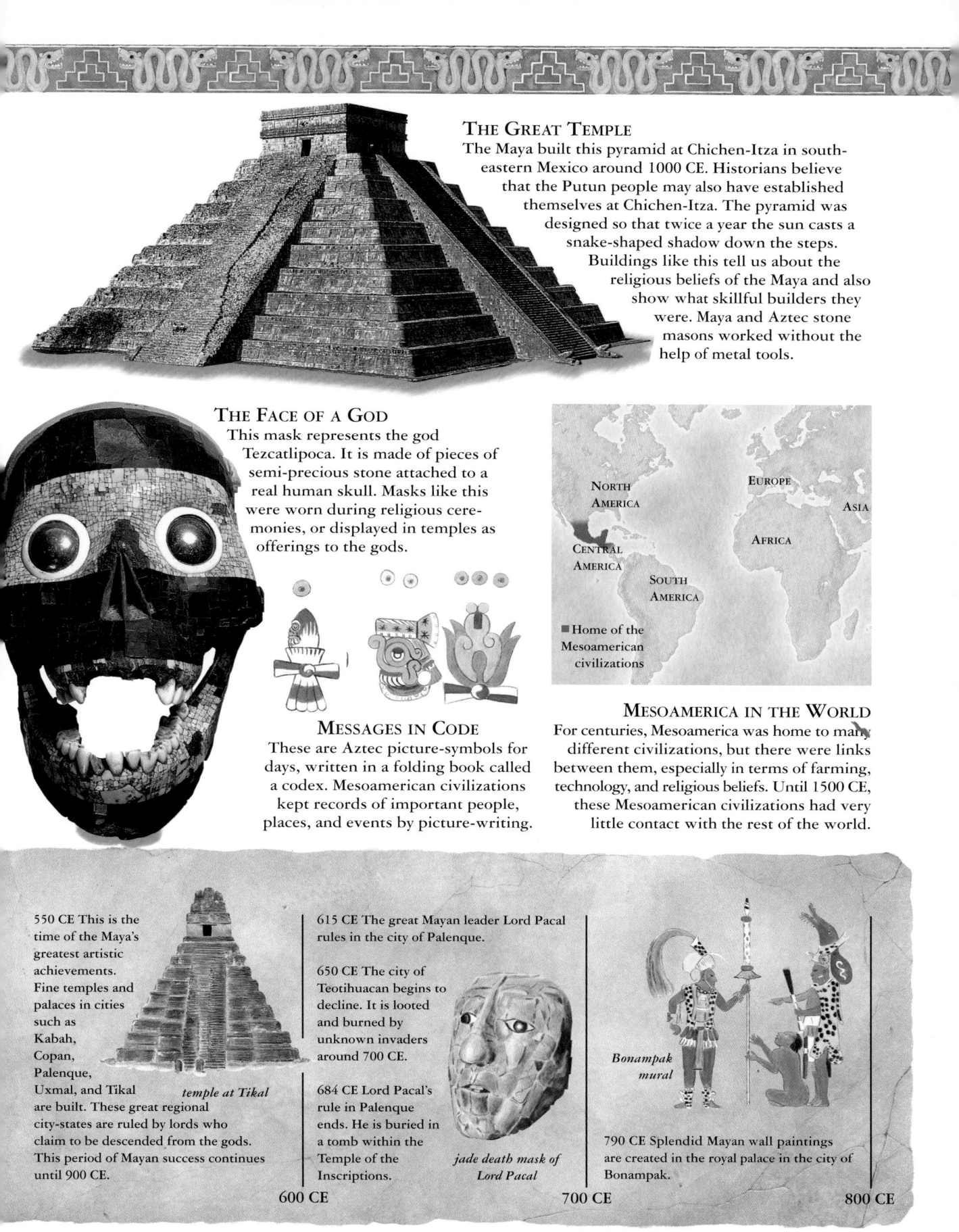

The Great Temple

The Maya built this pyramid at Chichen-Itza in southeastern Mexico around 1000 CE. Historians believe that the Putun people may also have established themselves at Chichen-Itza. The pyramid was designed so that twice a year the sun casts a snake-shaped shadow down the steps. Buildings like this tell us about the religious beliefs of the Maya and also show what skillful builders they were. Maya and Aztec stone masons worked without the help of metal tools.

The Face of a God

This mask represents the god Tezcatlipoca. It is made of pieces of semi-precious stone attached to a real human skull. Masks like this were worn during religious ceremonies, or displayed in temples as offerings to the gods.

Messages in Code

These are Aztec picture-symbols for days, written in a folding book called a codex. Mesoamerican civilizations kept records of important people, places, and events by picture-writing.

North America
Central America
South America
Europe
Asia
Africa
Home of the Mesoamerican civilizations

Mesoamerica in the World

For centuries, Mesoamerica was home to many different civilizations, but there were links between them, especially in terms of farming, technology, and religious beliefs. Until 1500 CE, these Mesoamerican civilizations had very little contact with the rest of the world.

550 CE This is the time of the Maya's greatest artistic achievements. Fine temples and palaces in cities such as Kabah, Copan, Palenque, Uxmal, and Tikal are built. These great regional city-states are ruled by lords who claim to be descended from the gods. This period of Mayan success continues until 900 CE.

temple at Tikal

615 CE The great Mayan leader Lord Pacal rules in the city of Palenque.

650 CE The city of Teotihuacan begins to decline. It is looted and burned by unknown invaders around 700 CE.

684 CE Lord Pacal's rule in Palenque ends. He is buried in a tomb within the Temple of the Inscriptions.

jade death mask of Lord Pacal

Bonampak mural

790 CE Splendid Mayan wall paintings are created in the royal palace in the city of Bonampak.

600 CE 700 CE 800 CE

Between North and South

MESOAMERICA IS A LAND of contrasts. There are high, jagged mountains, harsh deserts, and swampy lakes. In the north, volcanoes rumble. In the south, dense, steamy forests have constant rain for half the year. These features made traveling around difficult, and also restricted contact between the regions.

Mesoamerica was never ruled as a single, united country. For centuries it was divided into separate states, each based on a city that ruled the surrounding countryside. Different groups of people and their cities became rich and strong in turn, before their civilizations weakened and faded away.

Historians divide the Mesoamerican past into three main periods. In Preclassic times (2000 BCE–250 CE), the Olmecs were most powerful. The Classic era (250–900 CE) saw the rise of the Maya and the people living in the city of Teotihuacan. During the Postclassic era (900–1500 CE), the Toltecs, followed by the Aztecs, controlled the strongest states.

Each civilization had its own language, laws, traditions, and skills, but there were also many links between the separate states. They all built big cities and organized long-distance trade. They all practiced human sacrifice and worshipped the same family of gods. And, unlike all other ancient American people, they all measured time using their own holy calendar of 260 days.

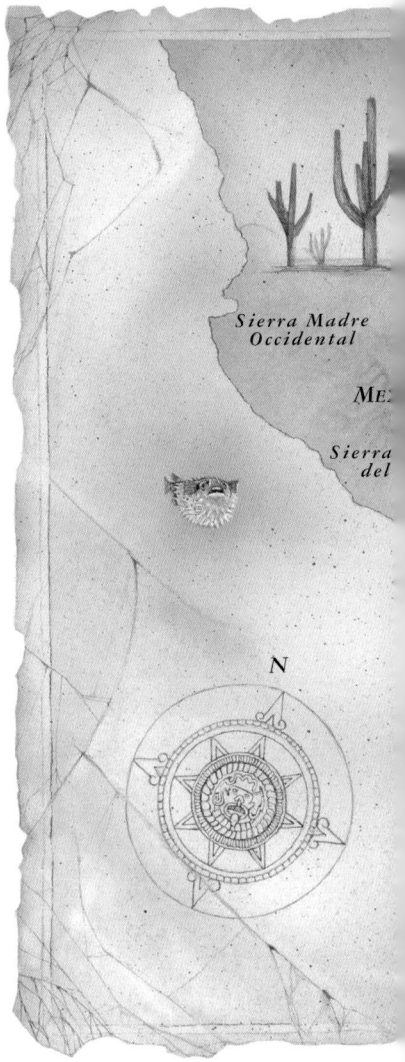

TIMELINE 800 CE–1400 CE

800 CE The Mayan palace-city of Palenque begins to decline.

856 CE The Toltecs of northern Mexico begin to create the city-state of Tula.

Palenque

900 CE Mayan power begins to collapse. Many Mayan cities, temples, and palaces are deserted and overgrown by the rainforest.
This is the beginning of the period known as the Postclassic era. The era lasts until 1500 CE.

950 CE The city of Tula becomes the center of fast-growing Toltec power.

986 CE According to legend, the Toltec god-king Quetzalcoatl leaves north Mexico for the Mayan lands of Yucatan.

Toltec warrior

1000 CE The Mayan city of Chichen-Itza becomes powerful. Historians believe that the Maya may have been helped by Putun warriors from the Gulf coast of Mexico.

1000 CE Toltec merchants do business along long-distance trade routes around the coast. They are helped by Mayan craftworkers. Long-distance trade has already been taking place in Mesoamerica for hundreds of years.

1011–1063 CE The Mixtecs are ruled by the leader Eight Deer, in the area of Oaxaca. The Mixtecs are master goldsmiths.

800 CE 900 CE 1000 CE 1100 C

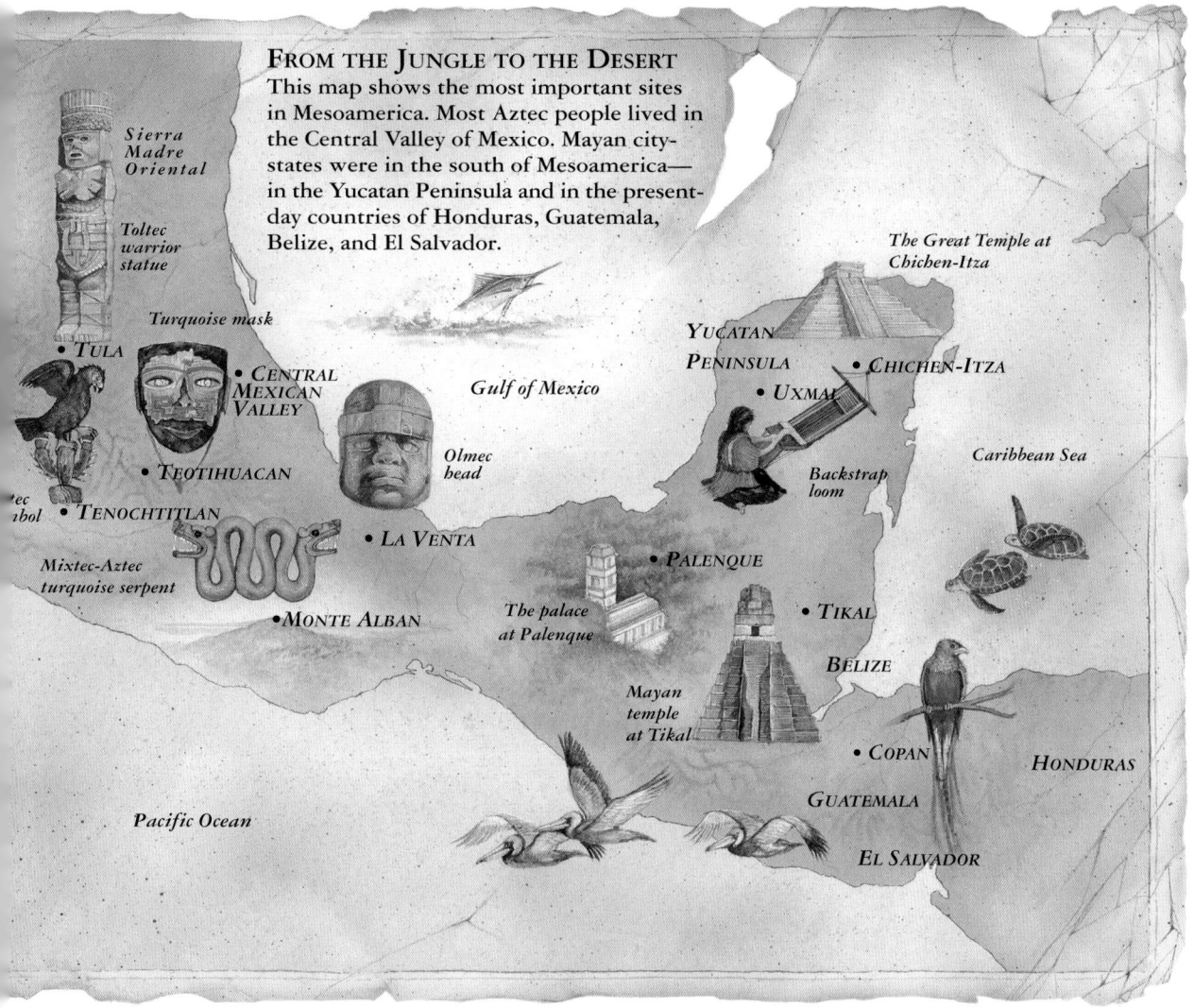

FROM THE JUNGLE TO THE DESERT
This map shows the most important sites in Mesoamerica. Most Aztec people lived in the Central Valley of Mexico. Mayan city-states were in the south of Mesoamerica—in the Yucatan Peninsula and in the present-day countries of Honduras, Guatemala, Belize, and El Salvador.

1100 CE Aztecs leave their homeland in the dry, semi-desert land to the north of Mexico and travel southward in search of a new place to live.

Aztec settlers

1168 CE The Chichimec people from central Mexico destroy the city of Tula and end Toltec power.

Aztec warrior

c. 1200 CE Aztecs arrive in central Mexico. They find Tepanecs, Culhuas, and Acolhuacans living there. At first, the Aztecs work as soldiers and slaves for these people, but they grow strong and fight against their masters.

c 1220 CE A new Mayan city is founded at Mayapan.

1300 CE The Mixtec civilization begins to thrive in Oaxaca, southern Mexico.

1325 CE Aztecs found the city of Tenochtitlan on an island in the center of Lake Texcoco, central Mexico.

1350 CE Aztecs begin to build *chinampas* (gardens) around Lake Texcoco.

1372–1391 CE The first-known Aztec ruler, Acamapichtli, reigns.

eagle on cactus, the symbol of Tenochtitlan

1200 CE 1300 CE 1400 CE

Famous People

FAME IN Mayan and Aztec times usually came with power. We know the names of powerful Aztec and Mayan rulers, and sometimes of their wives. However, very few ordinary people's names have been discovered.

Rulers' names were written in a codex or carved on a monument to record success in battle or other great achievements. Scribes also compiled family histories, in which rulers often claimed to be descended from gods. This gave them extra religious power. Aztec and Mayan rulers made sure their names lived on by building huge palaces, amazing temples, and tombs.

Some of the most famous Mesoamerican rulers lived at a time when their civilization was under threat from outsiders. Explorers from Europe have left us detailed accounts and descriptions of the rulers they met.

MAYAN RULER
This statue shows a ruler from the Mayan city of Kabah, in Mexico. Most Mayan statues were designed as symbols of power, rather than as lifelike portraits.

ROYAL TOMB
This pyramid-shaped temple was built to house the tomb of Lord Pacal. He ruled the Mayan city-state of Palenque from 615 to 684 CE. Its walls are decorated with scenes from Pacal's life.

TIMELINE 1400–1600 CE

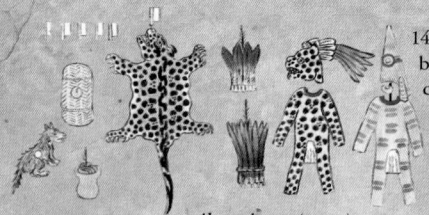

tribute items (taxes) collected by the Aztecs

1400–1425 CE The Aztec city of Tenochtitlan continues to thrive and grow.

1415–1426 CE The Aztec leader Chimalpopoca reigns.

1428 CE Aztecs defeat the Tepanecs and begin to conquer neighboring lands and collect tribute (taxes) from them.

1428 CE Aztecs set up the Triple Alliance. This was an agreement with neighboring city-states Texcoco and Tlacopan that made them the strongest force in Mexico.

1440 CE Moctezuma Ilhuicamina, the greatest Aztec ruler, begins his reign. He reigns until 1468.

1441 CE The Mayan city of Mayapan is destroyed by civil war.

1468 CE Aztec ruler Axayacatl reigns.

1473 CE The Aztecs conquer the rich market city of Tlatelolco in central Mexico.

market traders in the market city of Tlatelolco

1400 CE 1425 CE 1450 CE 1475 CE

Gold seeker

Soldier and explorer Hernan Cortes (1485–1547) came from a poor but noble Spanish family. After Columbus's voyages, many Spanish adventurers traveled to Mesoamerica and the Caribbean hoping to make their fortunes. Cortes sailed to Cuba and then, in 1519, went on to explore Mexico. His example inspired many treasure seekers. One such man, Francisco Pizarro, went on to conquer the Incas of Peru.

Between Two Worlds

Malintzin (*far right above*) was from a Mesoamerican state hostile to the Aztecs. She was of vital help to the Spanish conquerors because she spoke the Aztec language and quickly learned Spanish. The Spanish called her Doña Marina.

The Last Emperor

Aztec emperor Moctezuma II (*above right*) ruled from 1502 to 1520. He was the last emperor to control the Aztec lands. Moctezuma II was a powerful warrior and a good administrator, but he was tormented by gloomy prophecies and visions of disaster. He was captured when Cortes and his soldiers invaded the capital city of Tenochtitlan in 1519. The following year he was stoned in a riot while trying to plead with his own people.

1481–1486 CE Aztec ruler Tizoc reigns.

1486 CE Aztec ruler Ahuitzotl begins his reign.

1487 CE The Aztecs' Great Temple in Tenochtitlan is finished. Twenty thousand captives are sacrificed at a special ceremony to consecrate it (make it holy).

1492 CE The European explorer Christopher Columbus sails across the Atlantic Ocean to America.

Columbus lands

1500 CE

1502 CE Columbus sails along the coast of Mesoamerica and meets Mayan people.

a comet appears in the sky

1502–1520 CE Moctezuma II reigns. During his reign, a comet appears in the sky. Aztec astronomers fear that this, and other strange signs, mean the end of the world.

1519 CE Hernan Cortes, a Spanish soldier, arrives in Mexico. A year later, Cortes and his soldiers attack Tenochtitlan. Moctezuma II is killed.

1521 CE The Spanish destroy Tenochtitlan.

1525 CE

1525 CE Spain takes control of Aztec lands.

1527 CE Mayan lands are invaded by the Spanish.

1535 CE Mexico becomes a Spanish colony.

Spanish soldier

1600 CE War and European diseases wipe out 10 million Aztecs, leaving fewer than a million, but the Aztec language and many customs live on. By 1600 CE, between 75% and 90% of Mayan people are also dead, but Mayan skills, beliefs, and traditions survive.

1600 CE

The Order of Things

MESOAMERICAN CITY-STATES were ruled by leaders with three separate tasks. They were army commanders, lawmakers, and priests. Many rulers claimed to be descended from the gods. Rulers were almost always men. Mesoamerican women—especially among the Maya—had important religious duties but rarely took part in law-making or army life.

Mayan rulers were called *ahaw* (lord) or *mahk'ina* (great sun lord), and each city-state had its own royal family. The Aztec leader was called the *tlatoani* (speaker). Originally, he was elected from army commanders by the Aztec people. Later, he was chosen from the family of the previous ruler. He ruled all Aztec lands, helped by a deputy called *cihuacoatl* (snake woman), by nobles, and by army commanders. Priests observed the stars, looking for signs about the future, and held religious ceremonies.

Rulers, priests, and nobles made up a tiny part of society. Ordinary citizens were called *macehualtin*. Women looked after their families. Men were farmers, fishermen, or craftworkers. There were also thousands of slaves, who were criminals, enemy captives, or poor people who had given up their freedom in return for food and shelter.

OFFICIAL HELP
This Mayan clay figure shows a scribe at work. Well-trained officials, such as this scribe, helped Mesoamerican rulers by keeping careful records. Scribes also painted ceremonial pottery.

HONOR TO THE KING
Painted pottery vases like this were buried alongside powerful Mayan people. They show scenes from legends and royal palace life. Here, a lord presents tribute (taxes) to the king.

MAYAN NOBLEWOMAN
This terra-cotta figure of a Mayan noblewoman dates from between 600 and 900 CE. She is richly attired and protecting her face with a parasol. Women did not usually hold official positions of responsibility in Mesoamerican lands. Instead, queens and other noblewomen influenced their husbands by offering tactful suggestions and wise advice. Whether she was rich or poor, a woman's main duty was to provide children for her husband and to support him in all aspects of his work.

The Ruling Class

A noble is shown getting ready for a ceremony in this Aztec codex picture. Aztec nobles played an important part in government. They were chosen by rulers to be judges, army commanders, and officials. Nobles with government jobs paid no taxes and were given a free house to live in. Noblemen and women were born into ancient noble families, related to the rulers. It was, however, possible for an ordinary man to achieve higher rank if he fought very bravely in battle and captured four enemy soldiers alive.

War Leader

This Mayan stone carving shows ruler Shield Jaguar (*below left*) getting ready to lead his army in 724 CE. He is wearing a padded tunic and holding a knife in his right hand. His wife, Lady Xoc, is handing him his jaguar headdress. Mayan rulers also took part in religious ceremonies, where they offered drops of their blood to the gods to ask for their help.

Men at Work

Here, Aztec farmers are harvesting ripe ears of corn. This painting comes from the Florentine Codex. This 12-volume manuscript was made by a Spanish friar. Codex pictures like this tell us a lot about ordinary people's everyday lives. Notice how simply the farmers are dressed compared to the more powerful people on these pages.

The Court, Government, and Laws

THE REMAINS OF MANY splendid palaces survive in Mesoamerican lands. In the 1500s, European explorers described the vast palace of the Aztec ruler Moctezuma II in Tenochtitlan. It had banquet rooms big enough to seat 3,000 guests, private apartments, a library, a schoolroom, kitchens, stores, an arsenal for weapons, separate women's quarters, spectacular gardens, and a large zoo. Etiquette in the presence of the emperor was very strict. Captains of the royal bodyguard had to approach Moctezuma barefoot, with downcast eyes, making low bows and murmuring, "Lord, my lord, my great lord." When they left, they had to walk backward, keeping their gaze away from his face.

Palaces were not just rulers' homes. They were also official government headquarters where rulers greeted ambassadors from neighboring city-states and talked with advisors.

Rulers also had the power to make strict laws. Each city-state had its own courts, where formidable judges had the power of life and death over people brought before them.

ROYAL RECORD
Mayan rulers set up carved stone pillars in their cities to record major events during their reigns. These pillars are called stelae. This one celebrates a Mayan ruler in Copan, Honduras.

THE SEAT OF POWER
This carved jade ornament shows a seated Mayan king. Although Aztec and Mayan leaders had the final responsibility for decisions, they also relied on judges, officials, and scribes to help them rule.

MAKE A FEATHER FAN

You will need: pencil, thick cardboard, thin red cardboard, scissors, double-sided tape, green paper, feathers (real or paper), masking tape, colored felt, white glue and brush, paints, paintbrushes, bamboo cane, colored yarn, tape.

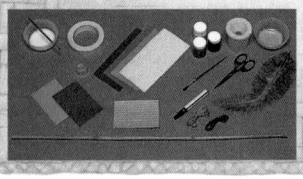

1 Draw two rings about 17 ¾ in. in diameter and 3 in. wide on thick cardboard. Cut them out. Make another ring the same size from thin red cardboard, as above.

2 Cut lots of leaf shapes from green paper. Stick them around the edge of one thick cardboard ring using double-sided tape. Add some real or paper feathers.

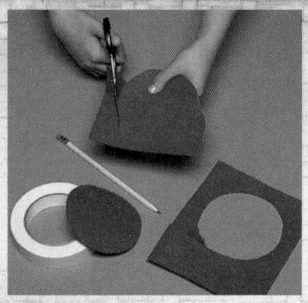

3 Cut two circles about 4 ¾ in. in diameter from thin red cardboard. Draw around something the right size, such as a roll of tape. These are for the center of the fan.

Locked Up

Here, a group of Aztec judges discusses how to punish two prisoners. You can see them cowering in a wooden cage. By modern standards, punishments were very severe. If ordinary citizens broke the law, they might be beaten or speared with cactus spines. For a second offense, they might be stoned to death.

The Rule of the Gods

This stone carving shows a human face being swallowed by a magic serpent. Royal and government buildings were often decorated with carvings such as this. They signified the religious power of the ruler of a particular city.

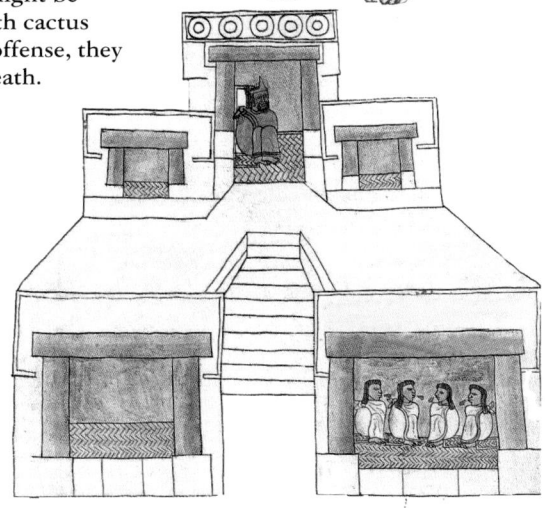

Fit for a King

This picture from an Aztec codex shows visitors to a ruler's palace. It was reported by Spanish explorers that over six hundred nobles came to the Aztec ruler's palace every day to attend council meetings, consult palace officials, ask favors of the ruler, and make their views heard. The ruler would sit on a mat on the floor with his council, as was the Aztec tradition.

Aztec nobles and rulers cooled themselves with beautiful feather fans.

4 Paint a flower on one of the two smaller red circles and a butterfly on the other. Cut V-shapes from the felt and glue them to the large red ring.

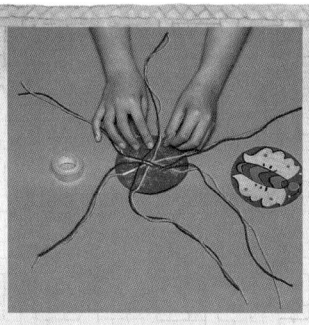

5 Using tape, attach lengths of colored yarn to the back of one of the red circles, as shown. Place the red circle in the center of the ring with leaves.

6 Tape the lengths of yarn to the outer ring to look like spokes. Coat the ring with white glue and place the second ring on top, putting a cane in between.

7 Use double-sided tape to stick the second red circle face up in the center. Glue the red ring with felt V-shapes on top of the second thick cardboard ring.

Family Life

FAMILIES WERE very important in Mayan and Aztec times. By working together, family members provided themselves with food, jobs, companionship, and a home. Each member of a family had special responsibilities. Men produced food or earned money to buy it. Women cared for babies and the home. From the age of about five or six, children were expected to do their share of the family's work by helping their parents. Because family life was so important, marriages were often arranged by a young couple's parents, or by a matchmaker. The role of matchmaker would be played by an old woman who knew both families well. Boys and girls got married when they were between 16 and 20 years old. The young couple usually lived in the boy's parents' home.

Aztec families belonged to local clan-groups, known as *calpulli*. Each *calpulli* chose its own leader, collected its own taxes, and built its own temple. It offered help to needy families, and kept a close eye on how its own members behaved. If a member broke the law, the whole clan might be punished for that person's actions.

MOTHER AND SON
These Mayan clay figures may show a mother and her son. Boys from noble families went to school at about 15. They learned reading, writing, math, astronomy, and religion.

PAINFUL PUNISHMENT
This codex painting shows a father holding his son over a fire of burning chiles as a punishment. Aztec parents used severe punishments in an attempt to make their children honest and obedient members of society.

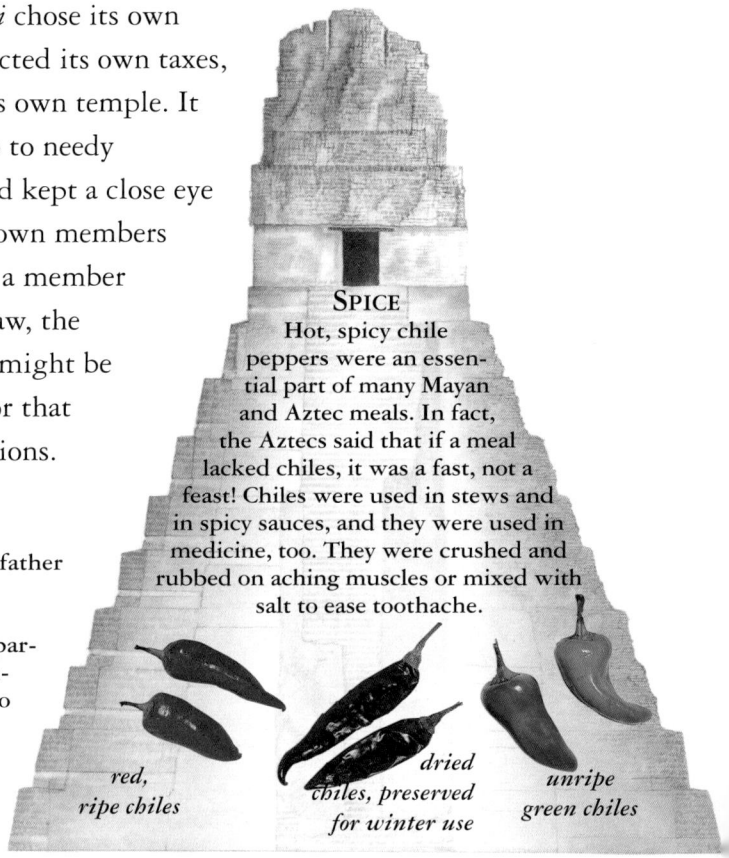

SPICE
Hot, spicy chile peppers were an essential part of many Mayan and Aztec meals. In fact, the Aztecs said that if a meal lacked chiles, it was a fast, not a feast! Chiles were used in stews and in spicy sauces, and they were used in medicine, too. They were crushed and rubbed on aching muscles or mixed with salt to ease toothache.

Ixtilton

This Aztec mask is made of a black volcanic stone called obsidian. It shows the god Ixtilton, helper of Huitzilopochtli, the Aztecs' special tribal god. Aztec legends told how Ixtilton could bring darkness and peaceful sleep to tired children.

Husband and Wife

The bride and groom in this codex picture of an Aztec wedding have their clothes tied together. This shows that their lives are now joined. Aztec weddings were celebrated with presents and feasting. Guests carried bunches of flowers, and the bride wore special makeup with her cheeks painted yellow or red. During the ceremony, the bride and groom sat side by side on a mat in front of the fire.

Guardian Goddess

The goddess Tlazolteotl is shown in this codex picture. She was the goddess of lust and sin. Tlazolteotl was also said to watch over mothers and young children. Childbirth was the most dangerous time in a woman's life, and women who died in childbirth were honored like brave soldiers.

Learning for Life

A mother teaches her young daughter to cook in this picture from an Aztec codex. The girl is making tortillas (flat corn pancakes). You can see her grinding the corn in a *metate* (grinding stone) using a *mano* (stone used with the *metate*). Aztec mothers and fathers trained their children in all the skills they would need to survive in adult life. Children from the families of craftworkers learned their parents' special skills.

In the Home

MESOAMERICAN HOMES were not just safe places to eat and sleep. They were workplaces, too. There were no refrigerators or household appliances, so women had to work hard preparing food for the day's meals or for winter storage. Vegetables were cleaned and chopped with stone knives, as there were no metal ones. Beans and chiles were spread out in the sun to dry, and corn kernels were ground into flour. Homes had to be kept clean as well. Firewood and water had to be fetched and clothes washed. Women and girls spent long hours spinning thread and weaving it into cloth, then sewing it into tunics and cloaks for the family. Some women wove cloth to sell or to give to the government as a tax payment.

Homes were also where most sick or elderly people were cared for.

HEART OF THE HOME
Throughout Mesoamerica, the hearth fire was the heart of the home. This charcoal burner shows Xiuhtecuhtli, the Aztec god of fire.

MAYAN POT
The Maya decorated ceremonial pottery with pictures of gods, kings, and important people. This pot shows a corn merchant. Pottery used in the home for food and drink would be less ornate.

A BACKSTRAP LOOM

You will need: paintbrush, water-based paint, 2 pieces of thick dowel about 2 ft. long, string, scissors, thick cardboard, masking tape, colored yarn.

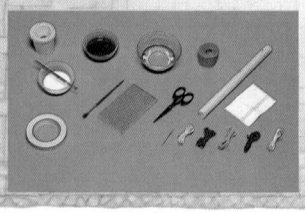

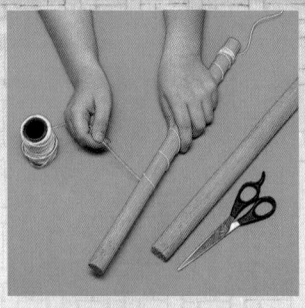

1 Paint the pieces of dowel brown. Leave them to dry. Tie string to each dowel and wind it around. Leave a length of string loose at each end.

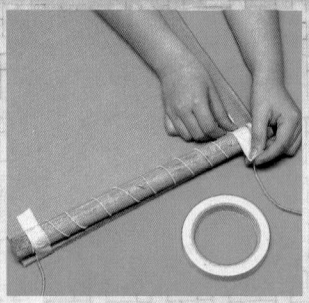

2 Cut a piece of thick cardboard about 27 in. x 40 in. This is a temporary base. Lightly tape the stringed dowels to it at the shorter sides with masking tape.

3 Now take your yellow yarn. Thread the yarn through the string loops and pull through to the other end, as shown. Try to keep the yellow yarn taut.

Glowing Colors

Many craftworkers worked at home. This painting by Diego Rivera shows craftworkers from the region of Tarascan dying hanks of yarn before they are woven into cloth. Mesoamerican dyes were made from fruits, flowers, shellfish, and the cochineal beetles that lived on cactus plants. Only rich people were allowed to wear clothes made from brightly colored cloth. Poorer people wore natural colors.

A Helping Hand

Aztec girls were expected to make themselves useful by helping their mothers at home. This Aztec codex picture shows a girl sweeping the floor with a bundle of twigs.

Weaving

Threads spun from plant fibers were woven into cloth on backstrap looms. The finest fabric was made from silky cotton. Rough yucca and cactus fibers made a coarser cloth. Looms like this are still used in Mexico today.

To weave, take the loom off the cardboard. Tie the loose string around your waist. Attach the other end of the loom to a post or tree with the string. Lean back to keep the long warp threads evenly taut.

4 Cut a rectangle of thick cardboard (12 in. x 1 ½ in). Now cut a small rectangle of cardboard with one pointed end, as shown. Wind red yarn around it.

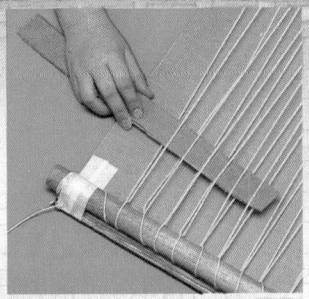

5 Now take your long cardboard rectangle. This is your shed rod. Carefully slide it through every second thread on your loom, as shown.

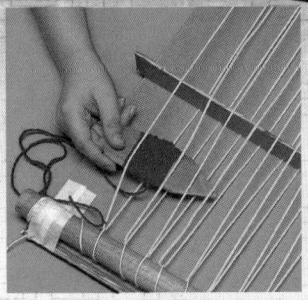

6 Turn your shed rod on its side. This will lift the threads up. Tie one end of your red yarn to the yellow wool. Feed the card of yarn through the lifted threads.

7 Lay the shed rod flat. Use the pointed end of your cardboard to pick up each of the first or alternate threads. Thread the yarn on the cardboard through these.

Villages and Towns

MOST PEOPLE in Mesoamerica lived in country villages. They made a living from the land, taking their produce to nearby market towns to sell. Villages and towns all had to obey the strongest city in the region. Usually they also had to pay a tribute (a tax of goods or labor) to it as well. Villages were small, often with fewer than fifty families, but the biggest cities were huge. Historians estimate that over 150,000 people lived in the city of Teotihuacan in 600 CE. Cities, towns, and villages were linked by roads cleared through the forest or by steep paths cut into mountain slopes.

The center of most Mesoamerican cities was dedicated to religion. The greatest temples stood there, close to a vast open space used for holy ceremonies, dances, and processions. Other important buildings, such as royal palaces and ball-courts, stood close by. The homes and workshops of ordinary citizens were built outside the ceremonial area.

HIDDEN IN THE TREES
Today, the remains of the great Mayan city of Tikal are almost hidden by the rainforest. In Mayan times, the trees would have been felled to make room for houses and fields. In around 800 CE, about 50,000 people lived here.

DESERT FRUITS
Several kinds of cactus thrive in Mexico's dry, semi-desert regions. The prickly pear is a sweet, juicy fruit, but the maguey cactus was even more popular. Its sap was used as a sweetener and to make an alcoholic drink. Its fibers were made into clothing and baskets. Its spines were used as needles.

BIG CITY
The Mayan city of Copan in present-day Honduras covered an enormous area, perhaps 8 mi. long and 2 mi. wide. The religious center and the nearby Great Plaza are shown here. Both were rebuilt in splendid style on the orders of King Yax Pac around 750 CE. The temples and royal palace are painted a glowing red—the color of life and power.

Birds of a Feather

These little pictures are from an Aztec codex. They show just some of the many beautiful wild birds that lived in Mesoamerica. The Maya and the Aztecs hunted many of them for their brightly colored feathers. These feathers could then be used to make fans or shields.

Mountains and Corn

On steep, cold mountain slopes, such as those of Popocatapetl, farmers grew hardy crops. *Chia* and *huautli* were both bushy plants with edible seeds. They were well suited to this environment. In sunny, fertile areas, corn was grown.

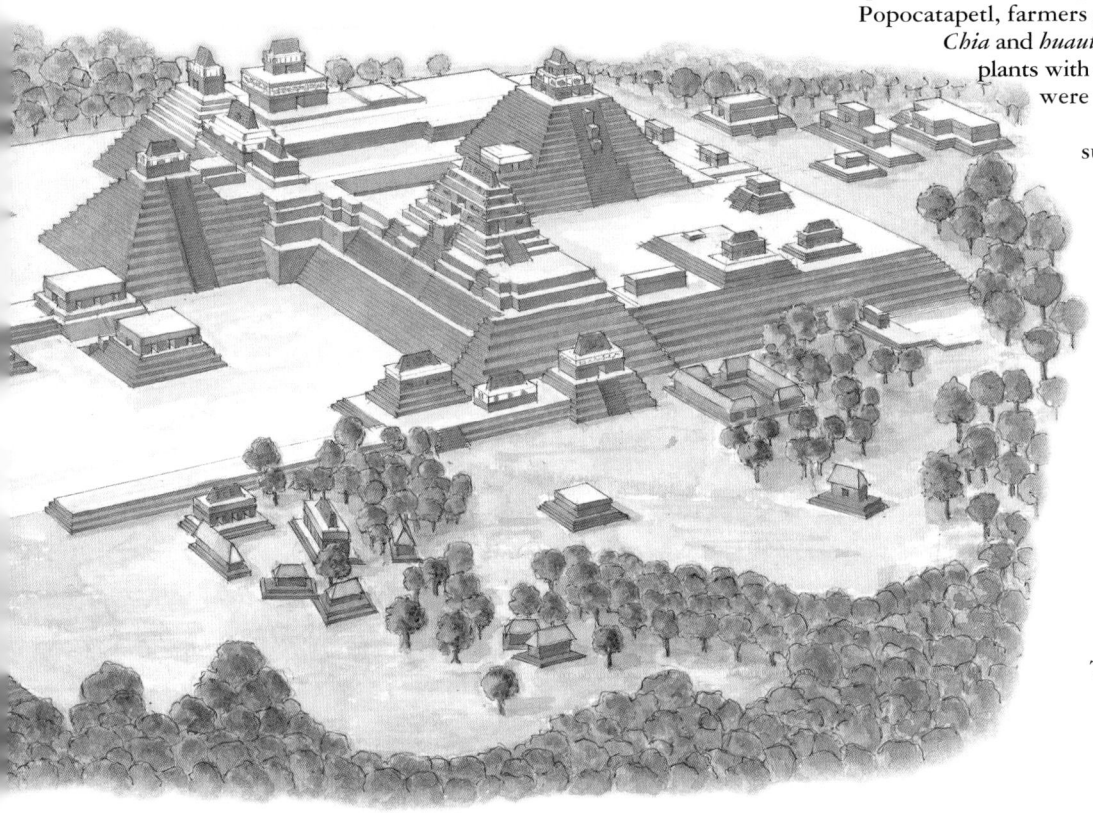

From Desert to Rainforest

The landscape of Mesoamerica is extremely varied. Many different creatures, from crocodiles to deer, inhabit it. The Maya and the Aztecs hunted many of these animals for their meat or skins.

Buildings and Houses

Family Home
This present-day Mayan family home is built in traditional style, with red-painted mud-and-timber walls. It has one door and no windows. The floor is made of pounded earth. The roof, thatched with dried grass, is steeply sloped so the rain runs off it.

People living in Mesoamerica used local materials for building. They had no wheeled transport, so carrying building materials long distances was quite difficult. Stone was the most expensive and longest-lasting building material. It was used for religious buildings, rulers' palaces, and tombs. The homes of ordinary people were built more quickly and easily of cheaper materials, such as sun-dried mud bricks, called adobe, or mud smeared over a framework of wooden poles. For strength, the walls might have stone foundations.

All Mesoamerican homes were very simply furnished. There were no chairs or tables, curtains or carpets—just some jars and baskets for storage and a few reed mats. Everyone, from rulers to slaves, sat and slept on mats on the floor. Most ordinary Aztec homes were L-shaped or built around a courtyard, with a separate bathroom for washing and a small shrine to the gods in the main room.

Buried Underground
Archaeologists have discovered these remains of houses at the Mayan city of Copan. The roofs, walls, and doors have rotted away, but we can still see the stone foundations. The houses are small and tightly packed together.

Make a Mayan House

You will need: thick cardboard, pencil, ruler, scissors, glue, masking tape, terra-cotta plaster paste (or thin plaster colored with paint), water container, wide gummed paper tape, paintbrush, balsa wood strips, short lengths of straw.

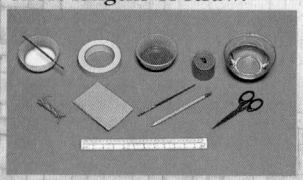

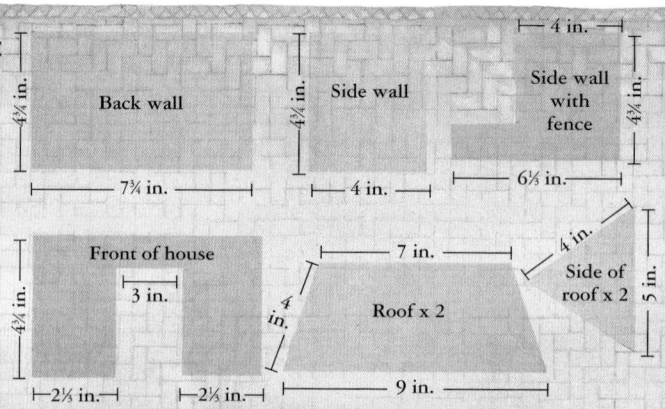

Draw the shapes of the roof and walls of the house onto thick cardboard, using the measurements shown. (Please note that the templates are not shown to scale.) Cut out the pieces.

1 Cut out a rectangle 10 in. x 6 in. from thick cardboard for the base. Stick the house walls and base together with glue. Use masking tape for support.

Stonemasons at Work

Mesoamerican masons constructed massive buildings using very simple equipment. Their wedges were made from wood, and their mallets and hammers were shaped from hard volcanic stone. Until around 900 CE, metal tools were unknown. Fine details were added by polishing stonework with wet sand.

Plaster

Big stone buildings, such as temples, were often covered with a kind of plaster called stucco. This was then painted with ornate designs. Plaster was made by burning limestone and mixing it with water and colored earth. By the 1400s, there was so much new building in Tenochtitlan that the surrounding lake became polluted with chemicals from the plaster making.

plaster

limestone

Skillful Stonework

This carved stone panel from the Mayan city of Chichen-Itza is decorated with a pattern of crosses. It was used to provide a fine surface for thick walls made of rubble and rough stone. This wall decorates a palace building.

A Mayan house provided a cool shelter from the very hot Mexican sun, as well as keeping out rain.

2 Paint the walls and base with plaster paste. This will make them look like sun-dried mud. You could also decorate the doorway with balsa wood strips.

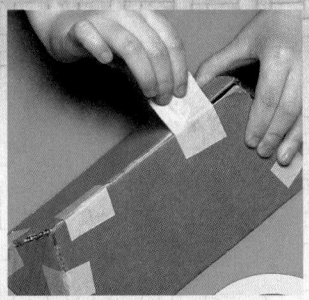

3 Put the house on one side to dry. Take your roof pieces and stick them together with glue. Use masking tape to support the roof, as shown.

4 Moisten the wide paper tape and use it to cover the joints between the roof pieces. There should be no gaps. Then cover the whole roof with glue.

5 Press lengths of straw into the glue on the roof. Work in layers, starting at the bottom. Overlap the layers. Attach the roof to the house using glue.

City in the Lake

THE AZTECS built their capital city, Tenochtitlan, on an island in the middle of Lake Texcoco in the Central Valley of Mexico. It was founded around 1325 CE and soon grew into one of the largest cities in the world. Historians estimate that over 200,000 people lived there by 1500. As the center of Aztec government, the city saw traders, ambassadors, scribes, and porters streaming in with huge loads of tribute (taxes) from all over Mesoamerica. Thousands of enemy soldiers captured in battle were also brought there to be sacrificed to the gods.

The city was divided into four districts—Flowery Place, Mosquito Fen, Herons' Home, and, at the center, the Sacred Precinct. The four districts of the city were linked to one another, and to the mainland, by countless little canals and causeways of pounded earth. These causeways ran above the surface of the lake. Fresh drinking water from the nearby mountains was carried by a tall stone acqueduct.

EAGLE AND CACTUS
According to legend, the Aztecs chose the site for Tenochtitlan after they received a message from the god Huitzilopochtli. He told them to build their city where they saw an eagle sitting on a cactus, eating a snake. Priests and rulers told stories like this to give reasons for their past actions and make people accept their future plans.

GIVING THANKS
The Aztecs decorated many parts of their city with images of their special god, Huitzilopochtli. Here we can see a brazier decorated with Huitzilopochtli's image, among the ruins of the great temple of Tenochtitlan.

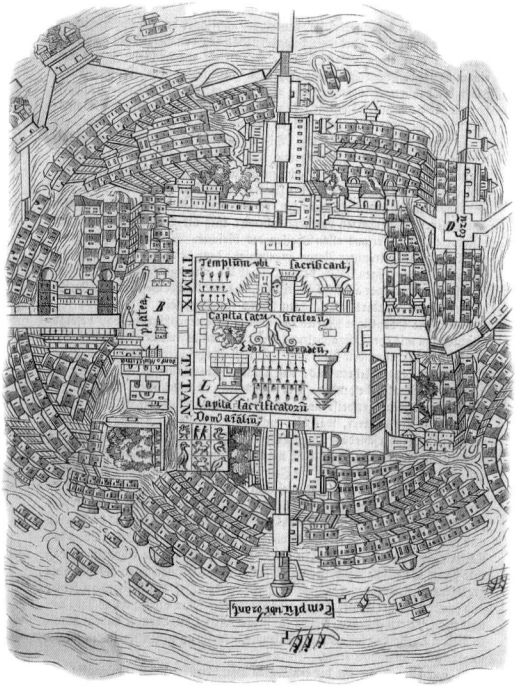

EYEWITNESS REPORTS
Today, Tenochtitlan is buried under modern Mexico City. However, we can gain some idea of what it was like from drawings like this one, made by a European artist in the 1500s. It shows how causeways and canals allowed easy movement around the city.

The Center of the City

The district called the Sacred Precinct was the ceremonial heart of Tenochtitlan. It housed huge temples. Compared with the small, crowded homes of ordinary people, the size of the buildings must have filled citizens and visitors with awe and fear. It was here too that hundreds of captives were brought to be sacrificed.

Stone Worshippers

These stone statues of standard bearers were found among the ruins of the Great Temple. This temple stood in the center of Tenochtitlan. It had two tall pyramids, topped by shrines. These shrines were dedicated to Tlaloc, god of rain, and Huitzilopochtli, the Aztec's own special god of war. The remains of steps leading up to these shrines can be seen today. When the Spanish conquered the city, they pulled down the Great Temple and built a cathedral near the site.

The Lake of the Moon

This is the name the Aztecs gave to Lake Texcoco. This fanciful picture shows an 18th-century artist's idea of the Aztec ruler, Tenoch. This ruler founded the city of Tenochtitlan.

Farming

PEOPLE LIVING in different regions of Mesoamerica used various methods to cultivate their land. Farmers in the rainforests grew corn, beans, and pumpkins in fields they cleared by slashing and burning. They cut down thick, tangled bushes and vines, leaving the tallest trees standing. Then they burned all the chopped-down bushes and planted seeds in the ashes. But the soil was only fertile for a few years. The fields were left to turn back into forest, and new ones were cleared. Mayan farmers also grew crops in raised fields. These were plots of land along the edge of rivers and streams, heaped with rich, fertile silt dug from the riverbed.

Aztec farmers planted corn wherever they could, on steep rocky hillsides and the flat valley floor. But they grew their biggest crops of fruit, flowers, and vegetables in gardens called *chinampas*. These were reclaimed from the marshy shallows along the shores of Lake Texcoco and around the island city of Tenochtitlan.

CORN GOD
This stone statue shows Yum Caax (Lord of the Forest Bushes), the Mayan god of corn. It was found at Copan. All Mesoamerican people honored corn goddesses or gods, as the crop was so important.

DIGGING STICKS
Mesoamerican farmers had no tractors, horses, or heavy plows to help them prepare their fields. Instead, a sharp-bladed wooden digging stick, called an *uictli*, was used for planting seeds and hoeing weeds. Some farmers in Mesoamerica today find digging sticks are more efficient than the kind of spade traditionally used in Europe.

FIELD WORK
This illustration by Bernardino de Sahagun shows Aztecs using digging sticks to plant fields of corn. If the May rains failed or frosts came early, a whole year's crop would be lost. Mesoamerican farmers made offerings to the rain god between March and October.

Chinampa soil was made even more fertile by using human manure.

Sticky mud was collected from the lake bottom. Along with compost and manure, this mud was poured on top of the chinampas.

The chinampa was held together by stakes, thick water vegetation, and the tangled roots of trees.

Floating Gardens

Chinampas were a sort of floating garden. They were made by sinking layers of twigs and branches under the surface of the lake and weighting them with stones. *Chinampas* were so productive that the government passed laws telling farmers when to sow seeds. This ensured there would be a steady supply of vegetables and flowers for sale in the market.

Slash and Burn

Mesoamerican farmers used a technique called slash and burn to clear land for farming. Crops grew very quickly in Mesoamerica's warm climate.

Vegetarians

Many ordinary Mesoamerican people survived on a largely vegetarian diet, based on corn and beans. This would be supplemented by other fresh fruits and vegetables in season. Meat and fish were expensive luxury foods. Only rulers and nobles could afford to eat them every day.

beans

prickly pear

Forest Fruits

This Aztec codex painting shows men and women gathering cocoa pods from trees. Cocoa was so valuable that it was sent as tribute to Tenochtitlan.

Hunting and Gathering

MESOAMERICAN FARMERS did not rear many animals to kill for food. Before the Spaniards arrived, there were no cows, sheep, pigs, or horses in their lands. Most meat and fish came from wild creatures, which were hunted or trapped. Deer, hares, rabbits, and foxes were hunted on the dry mountain slopes. Peccary (wild boar), armadillos, and opossums sheltered in the forests. Aztec hunters trapped ducks, geese, and pelicans in shallow reed beds beside the lake. Mayan fishermen caught turtles, dolphins, and shellfish all around the coast.

Hunters also went in search of many wild creatures that were not used for food. Millions of brightly colored birds were killed for their feathers. Poisonous snakes and fierce pumas, jaguars, and ocelots (wild cats) were hunted for their beautiful furs and skins.

Mesoamerican people also gathered a great many plants and insects for other uses. Seeds, leaves, bark, and flowers were used for medicine and to make paper, mats, and baskets. Wild bees supplied honey, and locusts were eaten as snacks.

INSECT HARVEST
Mesoamerican people collected many kinds of insects for use in medicines, as dyes, and as food. This codex picture shows cochineal beetles being gathered from a cactus. It took about 70,000 beetles to make two pounds of red dye.

HUNTERS
Mesoamerican men went hunting with bows and arrows, slings, clubs, and spears. Hunters' bows were made of wood, and their arrows were tipped with obsidian, a sharp volcanic glass. Their clubs were made from lumps of rock lashed to wooden handles with rope or leather thongs. To make their spears fly further, they used an *atlatl*. This was a grooved piece of wood that acted like an extra-long arm to increase the power behind the throw.

Chocolate Tree

This picture from an Aztec codex shows a cocoa tree and two Aztec gods. Cocoa pods could be gathered from cocoa trees all over Mesoamerica. Once ground, the cocoa beans were mixed with water to make chocolate. Chocolate was a highly prized drink and only nobles could afford to drink it. It was often sweetened with honey and flavored with vanilla. The Aztecs and Maya did not know how to make bars of solid chocolate, like those we enjoy today.

Fauna

Wild creatures such as turtles, and rabbits were abundant in Mesoamerica. Rabbits were hunted for their fur. Turtles were a popular catch for many fishermen. Their shells could be used in crafts, and their flesh could be eaten.

turtle

blacktail jackrabbit

Feathers

Mesoamerican merchants bought feathers from hunters who lived in the rainforest. The picture above shows different kinds of feathers sorted and ready for sale.

Sea Produce

This Mayan beaker is decorated with a picture of a god emerging from a shell. Beautiful seashells were highly prized in Mesoamerica and were often used in jewelry and craftwork. One species of shellfish was caught for its sticky slime. This slime was milked from the shellfish and then used to make a rich purple dye.

Rivers and Lakes

In this Aztec codex picture, we can see a boy fishing. He is standing in a flat-bottomed boat, hollowed from a single log. This boy is using a bag-shaped net, woven from cactus fiber. Fish were also caught with hooks, lines, and harpoons. Long nets, draped across canoes, were used to catch waterfowl.

Food and Drink

MESOAMERICAN PEOPLE usually had two meals a day. They ate their main meal around noon and a smaller snack in the evening. Ordinary people's food was plain and simple but very healthy—if they could get enough of it. When crops failed, there was famine.

Everyday meals were based on corn, beans, vegetables, and fruit. Peppers, tomatoes, pumpkins, and avocados were popular, but the Aztecs also ate boiled cactus leaves (with the spines removed). Gruel made from wild sage or amaranth seeds was also a favorite. Meat and fish were luxuries. Deer, rabbit, turkey, and dog were cooked for feasts, along with frogs, lizards, and turtles. The Aztecs also ate fish eggs and green algae from the lake.

USEFUL POTS

Mesoamerican people did not have metal cooking pots, so women cooked and served food in pottery bowls. Special pottery dishes were also used for specific jobs, such as cooking tortillas. The ones above were used for grating chiles and sweet bell peppers. They have rough-ridged bases.

CACTUS WINE

Sweet, sticky sap from the maguey cactus was collected in leather flasks, then left to ferment in open troughs. It quickly turned into a strong alcoholic wine, which the Aztecs called *pulque*. Aztec men and women were not usually allowed to drink much alcohol. On special festivals honoring the dead, *pulque* was served from huge pottery jars by women wine makers.

MAKE TORTILLAS

You will need: *scales, 8oz corn flour, 1 tsp salt, 1 1/2 oz butter, bowl, jug, 1/2 cup cold water, spoon, a little plain flour for kneading and flouring, rolling pin, pastry board, butter or oil for frying, frying pan.*

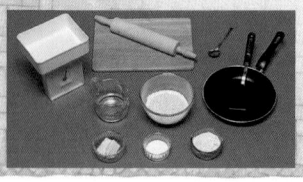

1 Carefully weigh out the ingredients. If you cannot find corn flour, use plain flour instead. Aztec cooks had to grind their own flour.

2 Mix the flour and salt together in a bowl. Rub the butter into the mixture with your fingers until it looks like bread crumbs. Then pour in the water.

3 Use your hands to mix everything together until you have a loose ball of dough. Do not worry if there is still some dry mixture on the sides.

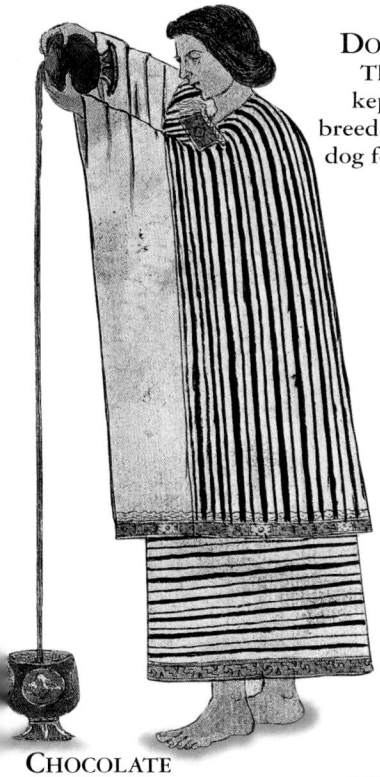

Chocolate
Mayan cooks dried and pounded cocoa pod seeds into a thick paste. This was then boiled with water. To make the mixture smooth and frothy, they poured it from one bowl to another, often from a great height.

Dog Food
The Aztecs kept several breeds of small dog for eating.

Tortillas and Tamales
This painting shows women grinding corn kernels into flour on a flat stone. They shaped balls of raw dough into pancakes (tortillas) and stuffed dumplings (tamales). Tortillas were cooked on a hot baking stone, while tamales were baked in a shallow dish.

New Food
In the years after the conquest of Mesoamerica, many vegetables were introduced to Europe, Asia, and the Middle East. At first, gardeners found them difficult to grow, and cooks did not know how to prepare them. But today, many meals include tomatoes, peppers, chiles, and avocados.

tomato

avocado

You could eat your tortillas with spicy bean stew and juicy tomatoes, just like the Aztecs did.

4 Knead the dough for at least 10 minutes until it is smooth. If the dough or your hands get too sticky, add a little plain flour to the bowl.

5 Transfer the dough out of the bowl to a floured pastry board. Divide it into egg-sized balls, using your hands or a knife. You should have about 12 balls.

6 Sprinkle the board and the rolling pin with a little plain flour to stop the dough from sticking. Then roll each ball of dough into a thin pancake shape.

7 Ask an adult to help you fry the tortillas, using a nonstick frying pan. Fry each tortilla for one minute per side. Use a little oil in the pan if you want to.

Keeping Healthy and Clear

MESOAMERICAN PEOPLE liked to keep themselves and their houses clean. They washed in river water, took baths, and swept their rooms with brushes of twigs and leaves. However, despite their attempts to stay clean and healthy, illness was common. Diseases recorded in Aztec lands, for example, include dysentery, chest infections, and skin complaints. Throughout Mesoamerica, children often died from infections or in accidents around the home. Women died in childbirth, and many men were killed in battle. People were considered old by the time they were 40.

Aztec medicine was a mixture of herbalism, religion, magic, and first aid. Aztec doctors gave out powerful herbal medicines and encouraged patients to say prayers and make offerings to the gods. Sometimes their cures worked, but often the patients died.

CACTUS TREATMENT
The Aztecs and Mayans used the pulp and juice of the prickly pear cactus to treat physical ailments, from digestive maladies to wounds and inflammations.

FOREIGN BODIES
Spanish settlers brought deadly diseases, such as measles and smallpox, to Mesoamerica after the conquest. Because of this the population of Central Mexico fell from around 12 million in 1519 to only one million in 1600.

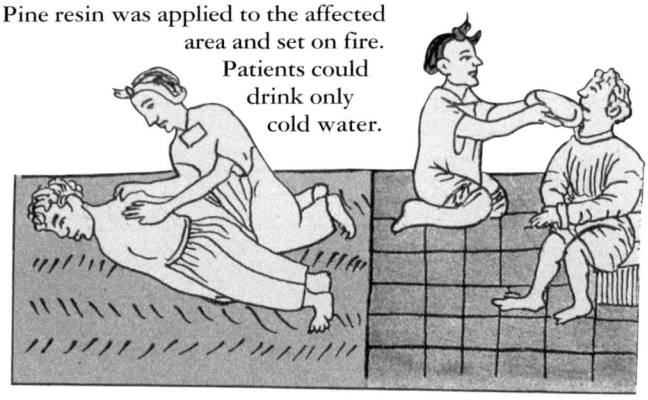

BURNING REMEDY
This scene from an Aztec codex advises people how to deal with fleas on their body. Pine resin was applied to the affected area and set on fire. Patients could drink only cold water.

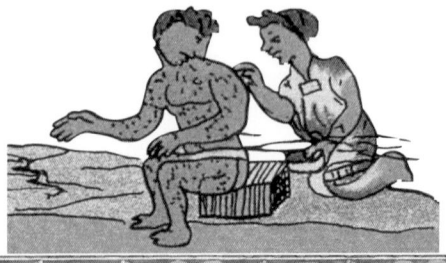

RASH MOMENT
A woman is shown treating an outbreak of sores on this man's skin. The patient would then drink and bathe in cactus sap.

Herbal Health

Many plants were cultivated or gathered for use in medicines. Their roots, seeds, leaves, and resin could be used.

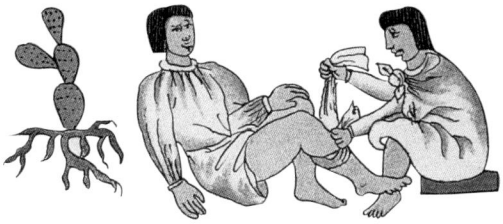

Break a Leg

To cure broken limbs, the Aztecs would grind various roots into a powder. These were placed on the break. A splint would then be tied to the broken limb.

After Care

The man shown here is recovering from a broken leg. After 20 days, a poultice of lime and powdered cactus root would be applied to his leg. When the leg was strong, the patient was advised to take a hot bath.

Deadly Bites

Many dangerous creatures lived in the deserts and rainforests of Mesoamerica. Bites from dangerous spiders and venomous snakes were common hazards. Herbal remedies, such as the roots of a tree called rabbit fern, were used to treat bites and stings.

Broken Skull

This man is suffering from a broken skull. The wound would be washed with urine to disinfect it.

Cough Mixture

A persistent cough could be cured by an infusion of *teouaxin* cooked with chile and salt.

Bathing Illness Away

Steam baths like this were used for keeping clean. The Aztecs also used them to try to cure illness. They believed the baths would drive out the evil spirits that caused many diseases. Steam baths worked like a present-day sauna. Bathers sat in a small cabin, close to a fire, which heated large stones. When the stones were very hot, water was poured over them, creating clouds of steam.

GLITTERING GOLD
This gold chest ornament is in the shape of a skeleton-faced god. It was made by Mixtec goldsmiths from southern Mexico. Jewelry was worn only by nobles. In Mesoamerica, both noblemen and women wore fine jewelry.

Clothes, Hairstyles, and Jewelry

AZTEC CLOTHES were very simple. Women wore a skirt and tunic, while men had a cloak and loincloth. But clothes still revealed a lot about the wearer. Strict laws described suitable clothing for different people. Ordinary families were meant to wear plain, knee-length clothes woven from rough *ixtle* (cactus fiber) and no jewelry. Nobles were allowed to wear longer-length clothes of fine white cotton, decorated with embroidery or woven patterns. They could also wear earrings, necklaces, labrets (lip-plugs), and bracelets of gold and precious stones. Mayan clothes were also simple—just strips of fabric wound around the body. Their ideas of beauty would be strange to us. They filed their teeth and encouraged their children to grow up cross-eyed. Mothers also bound their babies' heads to flatten them.

CEREMONIAL CLOTHES
Musicians and actors walk in procession in this picture. It is copied from a wall painting in a Mayan ruler's palace at Bonampak. The procession forms part of a celebration to honor the ruler's child. The men on the right are all wearing white cloth headdresses and wrap-around skirts, tied with sashes at the waist.

MAKE A BAT BROOCH

***You will need:** pencil, thin cardboard, scissors, black and gold paint, small paintbrush, paint container, palette, glue, glue brush, string, small safety pin, masking tape.*

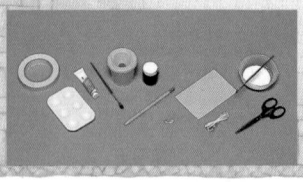

1 Draw the shape of your brooch in pencil on thin cardboard (2⅓ in. x 4 in.). This brooch is based on a gold Aztec pendant shaped like a vampire bat god.

2 Carefully cut out the finished shape with scissors. Aztec jewelry designs were very delicate and complicated. They often featured gods.

3 Use black paint to color in the eyes, mouth, and hair of your bat, as shown above. It is best to use the paint fairly thickly.

Cloak and Dagger

This Aztec warrior is wearing a long, brightly colored cloak and an elaborate feather headdress. Aztec cloaks were simple rectangles of cloth, fastened at the shoulder by a knot. There were strict rules governing their length. Only nobles or soldiers who had legs that had been badly scarred in battle could wear cloaks like this one, coming below the knee. Ordinary men had to wear short cloaks.

Mexican Style

A Huastec woman from Veracruz, on the north coast of Mexico, is shown in this statue. She is wearing a wide tunic and a long skirt. Her hair is tied up in a carefully folded headdress, and she wears a necklace and disk-shaped earrings. Although different patterns were favored by the peoples of the various Mesoamerican cultures, the style of clothing was essentially very similar.

Skirts, Tunics, and Cloaks

A well-off Aztec couple sit by the fire, while their hostess cooks a meal. Both women are wearing long skirts. The bright embroider of their tunics is a sign of high rank. Their long hair is braided and tied on top of their heads to make horns in a typical married woman's style. Girls and unmarried women wore their hair loose down their backs.

4 Cut teeth out of cardboard and glue in place. Use the glue to stick string on the bat's face, head, and body. Coil the string into spirals for the hair. Let brooch dry.

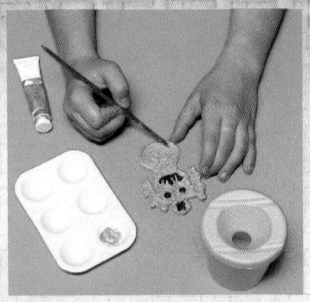

5 Carefully paint the brooch all over (except for the black areas) with gold paint. Let stand in a warm place for the paint to dry.

6 When the paint is dry, turn the brooch over and tape a safety pin on to the back with masking tape. Make sure it is secure.

You could wear your brooch on your chest, as the Aztecs did, or pin it on your sleeve.

Mosaic Mask
This ritual mask is inlaid with a mosaic of turquoise. This valuable stone was brought back from mines in North America by Aztec traders.

Craftworkers

Spanish explorers arriving in Mesoamerica were amazed at the wonderful objects they found there. They were different from anything they had seen in Europe. Pottery, jewelry, fabrics, mosaics, masks, knives, and feather work were all made by skilled Mesoamerican craftworkers using simple, hand-powered tools. In big cities such as Tenochtitlan, Aztec craftworkers organized themselves into guilds. These made sure that all members worked to the highest standards and trained new workers. Many craft skills were passed from parents to children. Sometimes whole families worked as a team in workshops next to the family home.

Many Mesoamerican craft goods were decorated with beautiful patterns. Often, they had special religious meanings. Aztec warriors marched into battle carrying magic feathered shields. Jewelry was decorated with death's-head designs. Many Mayan rulers and nobles were buried with elaborately decorated pots.

Living Jewels
Featherworkers wove or glued thousands of feathers together to make headdresses, cloaks, warriors' uniforms, shields, and fans. Men drew the designs on stiffened cloth and made light wooden frames to support the finished item. Women cleaned and sorted the feathers.

Make a Mosaic Mask

You will need: balloon, petroleum jelly, newspaper, papier-mâché mixture (1 part white glue to 3 parts water), bowl, paintbrush, scissors, palette of paints, container, self-drying clay, gummed paper tape, cardboard, plaster colored with paint.

1 Inflate a balloon to the size of your head. Cover with petroleum jelly. Soak strips of newspaper in papier-mâché mixture. Add five layers to the front of the balloon.

2 Once dry, pop the balloon. Draw a mask shape on to the papier-mâché and cut it out. Use clay to add eyes and a nose. Cover the edges with gummed paper tape. Let dry.

3 Mix white and blue paint to create three different shades. Paint one sheet of cardboard with each. When dry, cut them into little pieces.

WARRIOR DISH
This dish was made in the Mayan city of Tikal, (present-day Guatemala). It is painted with slip (a liquid clay colored with minerals) and shows the figure of a warrior. All Mesoamerican pots were shaped by hand—the potter's wheel was unknown.

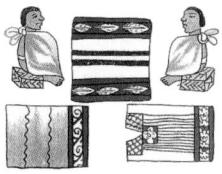

WEAVINGS
Cloaks and blankets were sent as tribute (taxes) to the great city of Tenochtitlan, as well as sold in markets.

TREASURES
Mesoamerican people treasured many beautiful semi-precious stones, such as turquoise, obsidian, and rock-crystal. They paid high prices for corals, pearls, and shells from the sea. But they valued jade, a hard, smooth, deep-green stone, most of all, because it symbolized eternal life.

turquoise

obsidian

MOLDING GOLD
This painting by Diego Rivera shows Aztec goldsmiths with molten gold. Most jewelry was made by melting gold dust in a furnace, then pouring it into a mold.

Aztec craftworkers carefully cut semi-precious stones into tiny squares. Turquoise, jade, shell, and obsidian were all used for this purpose. The craftworkers used these pieces to create beautiful mosaic masks like this.

4 Cover the mask (except the eyes and mouth) with plaster paste. Press the cardboard pieces into this, using glue to help any awkward ones stick.

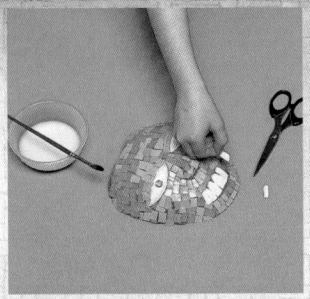

5 Paint the eyes with black and white paint. Cut out teeth from white cardboard and carefully glue in position. Leave the mask in a warm place to dry.

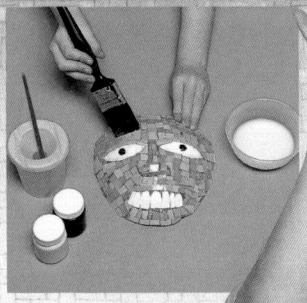

6 Now coat the whole mask with a thin coat of white glue. This will seal the surface of the mask.

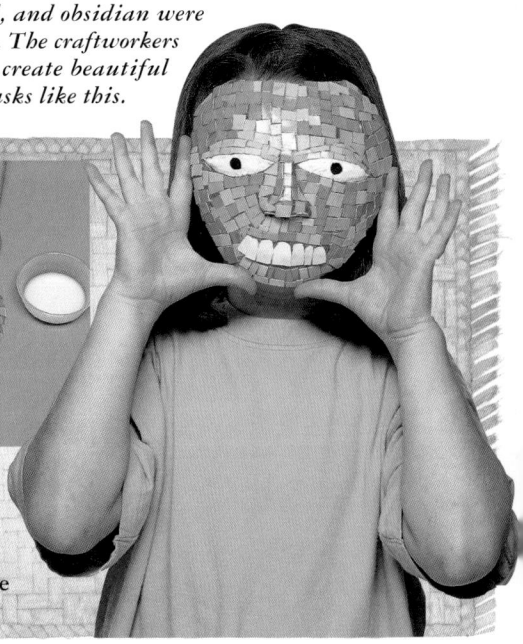

Merchants and Markets

THE MARKET PLACE was the heart of many Mesoamerican cities and towns. Traders, craftworkers, and farmers met there to exchange their produce. Many market traders were women. They sold cloth or cooking pots, made by themselves or their families, and corn, fruit, flowers, and vegetables grown by their husbands. In big cities, such as the trading center of Tlatelolco, government officials also sold exotic goods that had been sent to the Aztec rulers as tribute (taxes) by conquered city-states. After the Aztecs conquered Tlatelolco in 1473, it soon became the greatest market in Mesoamerica. It was reported that almost 50,000 people came there on the busiest days.

Long-distance trade was carried out by merchants called *pochteca.* Gangs of porters carried their goods. The work was often dangerous, but the rewards were great.

MERCHANT GOD
Yacatecuhtli was the Aztec god of merchants and traders. In the codex picture above, he is shown standing in front of a crossroads marked with footprints. Behind him (*right*), is a tired porter with a load of birds on his back.

CORN MARKET
Mesoamerican farmers grew many different varieties of corn, with cobs that were pale cream, bright yellow, or even deep blue. Their wives took the corn to market, as selling was women's work. This modern wall-painting shows Aztec women buying and selling corn in the great market at Tlatelolco. At the market, judges sat in raised booths, keeping a lookout for thieves and cheats.

MAKE A MAYAN POT

You will need: self-drying clay, board, rolling pin, masking tape, water bowl, small bowl, petroleum jelly, modeling tool, white glue, glue brush, yellow and black paint, paintbrush, water container.

1 Roll out the clay until it is approximately ¼ in. thick. Cut out a base for the pot with a modeling tool. Use a roll of masking tape as a guide for size.

2 Roll out some long sausages of clay. Coil them around the base of the pot to build up the sides. Join and smooth the clay with water as you go.

3 Model a lip at the top of the pot. Let it dry. Cover a small bowl with petroleum jelly. Make a lid by rolling out some clay. Place the clay over the bowl.

Journey's End
This modern painting shows merchants and porters arriving at the market city of Tlatelolco. Such travelers made long journeys to bring back valuable goods, such as shells, jade, and fig-bark paper. Young men joining the merchants' guild were warned about fatigue, pain, and ambushes on their travels.

Skins
Items such as puma, ocelot, and jaguar skins could fetch a high price at market.

Barter
Mesoamerican people did not have coins. They bought and sold by bartering, exchanging the goods they wanted to sell for other people's goods of equal value. Costly items such as gold dust, quetzal feathers, and cocoa beans were exchanged for goods they wanted to buy.

colorful feathers

cocoa beans

Market Produce
In Mexico today, many markets are still held on the same sites as ancient ones. Many of the same types of foodstuffs are on sale there. In this modern photograph, we see tomatoes, avocados, and other vegetables that were also grown in Aztec times. Today, as in the past, most market traders and shoppers are women.

Mesoamerican potters made their pots by these coil or slab techniques. The potter's wheel was not used at all in Mesoamerica. The pots were sold at the local market.

4 Turn your pot upside down and place it over the rolled-out clay. Trim the excess clay with a modeling tool by cutting around the top of the pot.

5 Use balls of clay to make a turtle to go on top of the lid. When both the lid and turtle are dry, use white glue to stick the turtle onto the center of the lid.

6 Roll three small balls of clay of exactly the same size for the pot's feet. When they are dry, glue them to the base of the pot. Make sure they are evenly spaced.

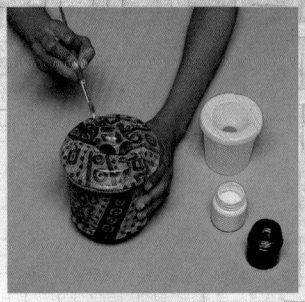

7 Paint the pot with Aztec designs in black and yellow. When you have finished, varnish the pot with a thin coat of white glue to make it shiny.

Travel and Transport

Carried High
A Mayan nobleman is shown being carried in a litter (portable bed) made from jaguar skins. Spanish travelers reported that the Aztec emperor was carried in the same way. Blankets were also spread in front of the emperor as he walked, to keep his feet from touching the ground.

Mesoamerican people knew about wheels, but they did not make wheeled transport of any kind. Carriages and carts would not have been suitable for journeys through dense rainforests or along steep, narrow mountain tracks. Many Mayan cities were also linked by raised causeways that would have been difficult for wheeled vehicles to travel along.

Most people traveled overland on foot, carrying goods on their backs. Mesoamerican porters carried heavy loads with the help of a *tumpline*. This was a broad band of cloth that went across their foreheads and under the bundles on their backs, leaving their arms free. Rulers and nobles were carried in beds, called litters.

On rivers and lakes, Mesoamericans used simple dug-out boats. At sea, Mayan sailors traveled in huge wooden canoes that were able to make voyages of many miles in rough seas.

Men or Monsters?
Until the Spaniards arrived with horses in 1519, there were no animals big and strong enough to ride in the Mesoamerican lands. There were horses in America in prehistoric times, but they died out around 10,000 BCE. When the Aztecs saw the Spanish riding horses, they thought they were monsters—half man, half beast.

A Wheeled Dog

You will need: a board, self-drying clay, 4 lengths of thin dowel about 2 in. long and 2 lengths about 2¾ in. long, thick cardboard, scissors, water bowl, board, modeling tool, paintbrush, white glue, paint container, masking tape.

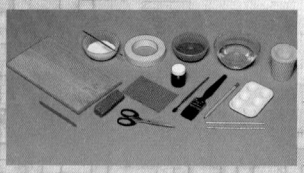

1 Roll a large piece of clay into a fat sausage to form the dog's body. Push the 2 in. pieces of dowel into the body to make the legs. Let dry.

2 Cover the dowel legs with clay, extending the clay ¾ in. beyond the end of the dowel. Make a hole at the end of each leg with a piece of dowel. Let dry.

3 Push the dowel through the holes in the legs to join them horizontally. Make the dog's head and ears from clay. Attach them to the body using water.

Hardworking Porters

This engraving from the 1900s shows Aztec slaves and commoners carrying loads for Spanish conquerors. Being a porter was very hard work. They were expected to cover up to 62 mi. per day, carrying about 55–66 lbs. on their backs. Like most Mesoamerican people, they traveled these long distances barefoot.

By Boat

Aztec soldiers and the citizens of Tenochtitlan used boats with flat bottoms to travel around the city. Boats like this were also used to carry fruits and vegetables to market. Dug-out canoes were popular, too. They were made from hollowed-out tree trunks.

Aztec Waterways

The Aztecs paddled their canoes and flat-bottomed boats on Lake Texcoco. Today most of this lake has dried up. The lakeside *chinampas*, where they grew food and flowers, have almost disappeared. This photograph shows modern punts sailing along one of the last remaining Aztec waterways between the few *chinampas* that survive.

Toys like this dog are proof that the wheel was known in Mesoamerica. Wheeled vehicles were not suitable for rugged Mesoamerican land.

4 Cut four circles 1½ in. in diameter from cardboard to make wheels. Pierce a hole in the center of each. Make the holes big enough for the dowel to fit through.

5 Make four wheels from clay, the same size as the cardboard wheels. Glue the clay and cardboard wheels together. Make holes through the clay wheels and let dry.

6 Paint the dog's head, body, legs, and wheels with Aztec patterns. When the paint is dry, give the dog a thin coat of white glue to act as a varnish.

7 Put the wheels on the ends of the dowels that pass through the dog's legs. Wrap strips of masking tape around the ends to stop the wheels from falling off.

Warriors and Weapons

AZTEC ARMIES were very large. All Aztec men learned how to fight and had to be ready to hurry off to battle when they heard the sound of the great war drum outside the ruler's palace in Tenochtitlan. Ordinary soldiers wore tunics and leg-guards of padded cotton that had been soaked in saltwater. This made it tough—strong enough to protect the wearer from many fierce blows. Aztec army commanders wore splendid uniforms decorated with gold, silver, feathers, and fur.

Both the Maya and the Aztecs greatly admired bravery. Aztec armies were led by nobles who had won promotion for brave deeds in battle or for taking lots of captives. It was a disgrace for an Aztec soldier to try to save his own skin. It was more honorable for him to be killed fighting, or to be sacrificed, than to survive.

Mayan soldiers went to war to win captives for sacrifice, but they also fought battles to control trade routes, to obtain tribute, and to gain power. They wore a variety of garments, including sleeveless tunics, loincloths, fur garments, and cotton armor.

TOLTEC WARRIORS
A proud warrior stands at Tula, the capital city of the Toltec people. He wears a butterfly-shaped breastplate. Butterflies have short but brilliant lives. For the Toltecs, they were a symbol of brave warriors and early death. The Toltecs were famous for their battle skills throughout Aztec and Mayan lands.

HELD CAPTIVE
An Aztec warrior is shown capturing an enemy in battle in this codex picture. The warrior is dragging his captive along by the hair. Young Aztec men had to grow their hair long at the back and could only cut it when they had taken their first prisoner in battle.

AN EAGLE HELMET

You will need: ruler, thick cardboard, pencil, scissors, masking tape, stapler, self-drying clay, white glue, glue brush, gummed paper tape, paints, paintbrush, water container, ribbon, felt, green paper, Velcro.

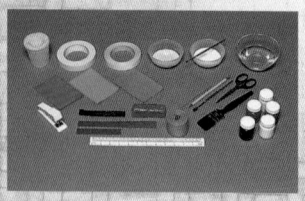

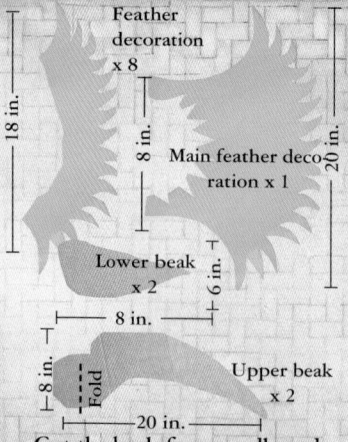

Cut the beak from cardboard. Cut the feathers from paper.

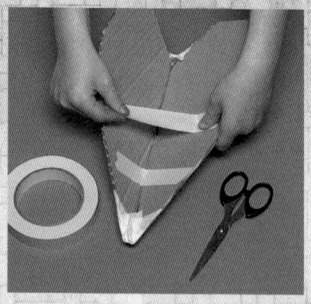

1 Make your helmet by joining the two parts of the upper beak with masking tape. Join the two parts of the lower beak in the same way, as shown.

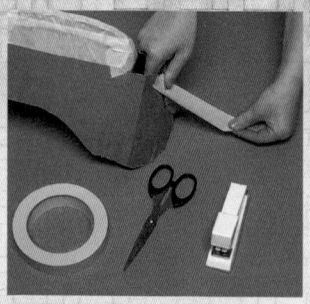

2 Fold the two rounded ends of the upper beak toward each other and staple them together. Cover the staples and the seam with masking tape.

Jaguar and Eagle Knights

Ocelotl, the jaguar, is shown in this picture from a codex. Warriors had to prove their bravery in battle and capture lots of prisoners for sacrifice. Those who succeeded were invited to join special fighting brotherhoods of jaguar and eagle knights. They wore costumes made of real feathers and skins.

Clubs and Spears

Aztec soldiers face Spanish soldiers on horseback. They are armed with war clubs called *macuahuitl* and are protected by wooden shields. War clubs, made of wood and razor-sharp flakes of obsidian, could cut an enemy's head off with a single blow. The Spaniards are armed with metal swords and lances.

Warrior Spirit

This stone carving is from the Mayan city of Yaxchilan. In it, Lady Xoc, wife of ruler Shield Jaguar, kneels before a vision serpent. This serpent was made to appear by a special religious ritual. Mayan rulers made offerings of their own blood to their ancestor spirits and to the gods to ask for help in battle.

Fasten your eagle helmet by tying it under the chin. You can make wings from cardboard and attach them to your arms with ribbon. Now you are a brave eagle knight! Eagles were admired by the Aztecs as superb hunters who could move freely to the sun.

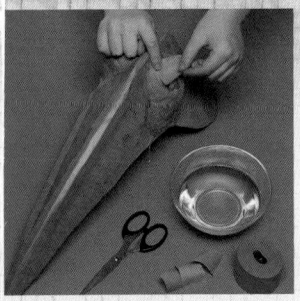

3 Make two eyes from self-drying clay and stick them on the upper beak with glue. Neaten the edges of the beak and eyes with gummed paper tape.

4 Decorate both parts of the beak with paint. If desired add pieces of ribbon, felt, or paper, too. Remember that you want to look brave and fierce.

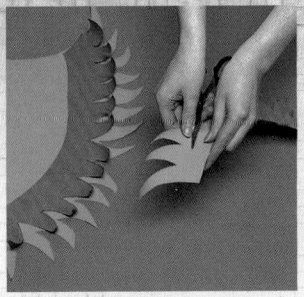

5 Ask an adult to curl the feathers by running a scissor blade along them. Glue the layers of feathers onto the main feather decoration. Trim to fit.

6 Use tape and glue to attach feathers to the inside of the upper beak. Tape ribbon from the upper beak to the lower one to join. Leave some ribbon loose to tie.

Rival City-States

THE MAYA LIVED in many separate city-states, which were always rivals and sometimes at war. Rulers of different states fought to win more land. From around 200 CE, they also competed with one another to fill their cities with bigger, more beautiful buildings. They competed over political power, control of land and resources, and trade routes.

Between about 850 and 900 CE, many Mayan cities became poorer, and their power collapsed. The great city centers were abandoned, and Mayan scribes and craftworkers no longer carved important dates on temples and tombs. The last date documented is 889 CE. No one knows why this happened. Perhaps it was because of famine, bad weather, or farmers over-using the land, or it may have been the result of war. However, Mayan civilization did not totally disappear. A few Mayan cities, in the far north and south of Mexico, continued to thrive.

Around 900 CE, the Putun people from the Gulf coast moved into Mayan lands. In cities like Chichen-Itza, Putun ideas blended with Mayan traditions to create a new culture.

TIKAL
This figure was painted on a pottery vase from the city of Tikal. From about 600 to 900 CE, Tikal was the greatest Mayan city-state. It was wealthy, busy, and very big. About 75,000 people lived there, and its buildings covered an area of 39 square miles. Around 400 CE, Tikal conquered the nearby Mayan state of Uaxactun. Trading and religious links were then developed with the powerful non-Mayan city of Teotihuacan.

CHICHEN-ITZA
Pilgrims came from miles around to throw jewelry and fine pottery into the Well of Sacrifice in the city of Chichen-Itza. These items were offerings to the god of rain. Human sacrifices were made here, too. Chichen-Itza was founded by the Maya around 800 CE. Later, Mayan craftsmen built a massive new city center, with temples and ball-courts. Many of these new buildings were based on designs similar to those found in central Mexico. Some historians think this means that the city was conquered by the Putuns.

Names and Dates

This stone slab was once placed above a doorway in the Mayan city of Yaxchilan. It is carved with glyphs, or picture-symbols, recording important names and dates. The city of Yaxchilan is famous for the fine quality stone carvings found there, especially on tall pillars and around doors.

Uxmal

The city of Uxmal is in the dry Puuc region of Yucatan, Mexico. There are no rivers or streams in the area, so Mayan engineers designed and built huge underground tanks, called *chultun*, to store summer rainfall. People living in Uxmal relied on these water tanks for survival.

Palenque

Lord Pacal, ruler of the Mayan city of Palenque, was buried wearing this mask of green jade. Only the richest city-states could afford to bury their rulers with treasures like this. Palenque was at its strongest between 600 and 800 CE.

Copan

This stela (tall stone pillar) is from Copan (in modern Honduras). Copan was the southernmost Mayan city. The front of the stela is carved with a larger-than-life portrait of 18 Rabbit (Waxaklahun ubah k'awil), the thirteenth ruler of the city. Archaeologists know much about Copan's past from the inscriptions carved in several monuments and buildings.

TOTONAC TRIBUTE
Ambassadors from lands conquered by the Aztecs came to Tenochtitlan to deliver the tribute (taxes) demanded by their new rulers. This painting shows splendidly dressed representatives of the Totonac people meeting Aztec tax collectors. The Totonacs lived on the Gulf coast of Mexico, in Veracruz. Here they are shown offering tobacco, fruit, and vanilla grown on their lands. They hated and feared the Aztecs.

Aztec Conquests

WAR WAS ESSENTIAL to Aztec life. As newcomers in Mexico, the Aztecs had won their homeland by fighting against the people already living there. From then onward, they relied on war to bring more land, new cities, and tribute (taxes) under their control. Without these riches won through war, the Aztec empire would have collapsed. Big cities such as Tenochtitlan needed steady supplies of tribute to feed their citizens. War was also a source of captives. The Aztecs believed that thousands of prisoners needed to be sacrificed each year.

Each new Aztec ruler had to start his reign with a battle. It was his duty to win fame and glory by conquering new territory and seizing enemy captives. During the 1400s, the Aztec empire grew rapidly, until the Aztecs ruled most of Mexico. This drive to conquer new territory was led by rulers Itzcoatl (1426–1440), Moctezuma Ilhuicamina (1440–1468), and Axayacatl (1468–1481). Conquered cities were often controlled by garrisons of Aztec soldiers and linked to the government in Tenochtitlan by large numbers of officials, such as tax collectors and scribes.

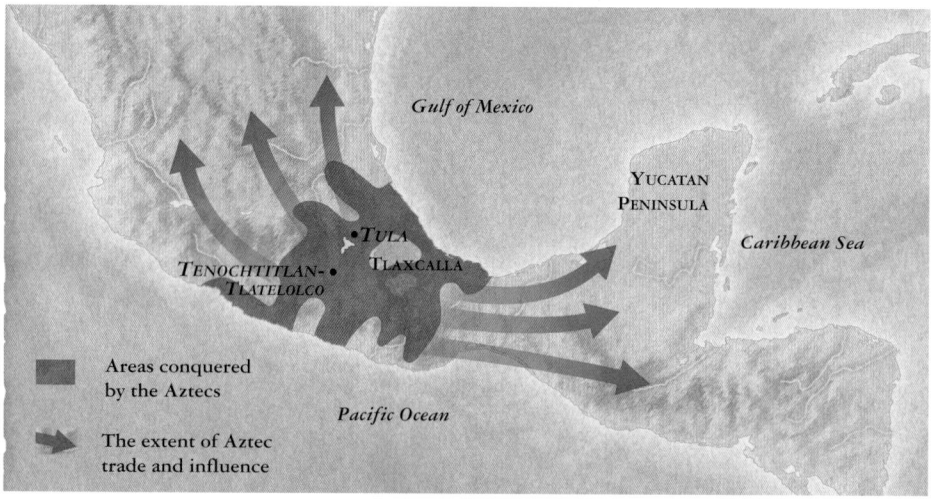

AZTEC LANDS
This map shows the area ruled by the Aztecs in 1519. Conquered cities were allowed to continue with their traditional way of life but had to pay tribute to Aztec officials. The Aztecs also put pressure on two weaker city states, Texcoco and Tlacopan, to join with them in a Triple Alliance. One nearby city-state, Tlaxcalla (see map), refused to make an alliance with the Aztecs and stayed fiercely independent.

Cannibals

One of the Aztecs' most important reasons for fighting was to capture prisoners for sacrifice. In this codex picture, we can see sacrificed bodies neatly chopped up. In some religious ceremonies, the Aztecs ate the arms and legs of sacrificed prisoners.

From Humble Beginnings

Aztec settlers are shown on their difficult trek through northern Mexico. The Aztecs built up their empire from humble beginnings in a short time. They first arrived in Mexico some time after 1200 CE. By around 1400, they had become the strongest nation in central Mesoamerica. To maintain their position, they had to be ready for war. The Aztecs invented many legends to justify their success. They claimed to be descended from earlier peoples living in Mexico, and to be specially guided by the gods.

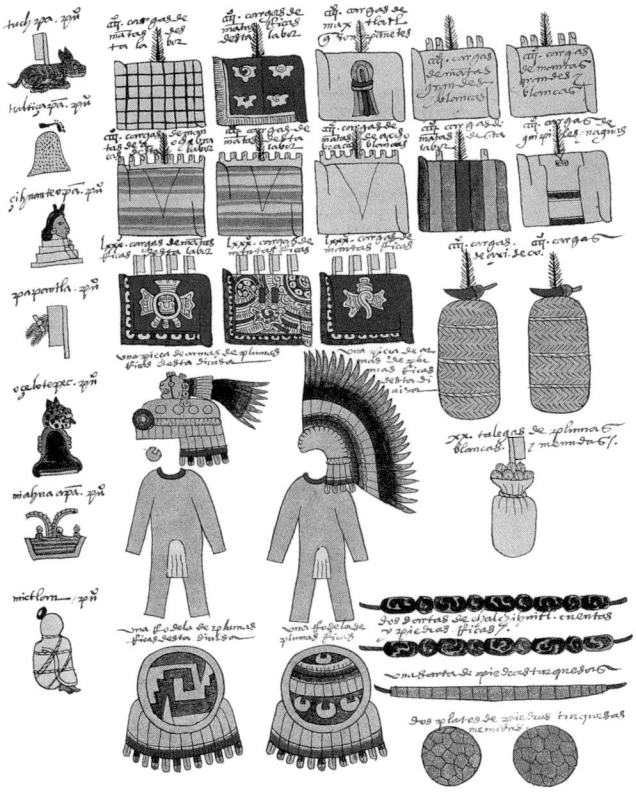

Tribute List

The Aztecs received vast quantities of valuable goods as tribute (taxes) each year. Most of the tribute was sent to their capital city of Tenochtitlan. Aztec scribes there drew up very detailed lists of tribute received, like the one on the left. Among the goods shown are shields decorated with feathers, blankets, turquoise plates, bracelets, and dried chile peppers.

Scholars and Scribes

THE MAYA were the first—and only—Native American people to invent a complete writing system. Mayan picture-symbols and sound-symbols were written in books, carved on buildings, painted on pottery, and inscribed on precious stones. Mayan scribes also developed an advanced number system, including a sign for zero, which Europeans at the time did not have. Mayan writing used glyphs (pictures standing for words) and also picture-signs that stood for sounds. The sound-signs could be joined together, like the letters of our alphabet, to spell out words and to make complete sentences. The Aztecs used picture-writing too, but theirs was much simpler and less flexible.

Mayan and Aztec picture-symbols were very difficult to learn. Only specially trained scribes could write them and only priests or rich people could read them. They could spare time for study and afford to pay a good teacher.

MAYAN READER
This Mayan statue shows a wealthy woman, seated cross-legged with a codex (folding book), on her lap. A Mayan or Aztec codex was made of long strips of fig-bark paper, folded like an accordion. The writing was read from top to bottom and left to right.

CITY EMBLEM
This is the emblem-glyph for the Mayan city-state of Copan. It is made up of four separate images, which together give a message meaning "the home of the rulers of the royal blood of Copan." At the bottom, you can see a bat, the special picture-sign for the city.

MAKE A CODEX

You will need: thin cardboard, ruler, pencil, scissors, white acrylic paint, eraser, large and small paintbrushes, water container, paints in red, yellow, blue, and black, palette, tracing paper.

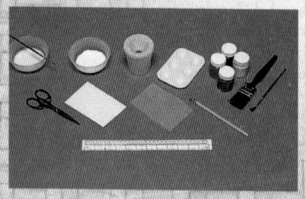

1 Draw a rectangle about 40 in. x 10 in. onto thin cardboard. Cut out the rectangle, Cover it evenly with white acrylic paint. Let it dry.

2 Using a pencil and ruler, lightly draw in four fold-lines 8 in. apart. This will divide the painted cardboard into five equal sections.

3 Carefully fold along the pencil lines to make a zig-zag book, as shown. Unfold the cardboard and rub out the pencil lines with an eraser.

Aztec Encyclopedia

These pictures of Aztec gods come from a book known as the Florentine Codex. This encyclopedia was compiled between 1547 and 1569 by Father Bernardino de Sahagun, a Spanish friar. He was fascinated by Aztec civilization and wanted to record it before it disappeared. This codex is the most complete written record of Aztec life we have.

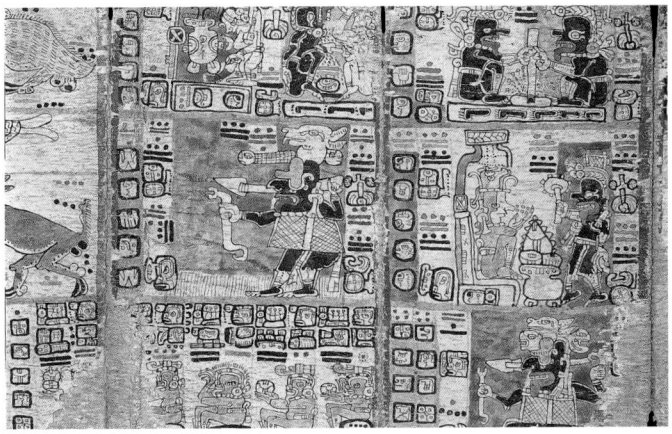

Mayan Codex

Mayan scribes wrote thousands of codices, but only four survive. All the rest were destroyed by Spanish missionaries. These pages from a Mayan codex show the activities of several different gods. The figure at the top painted black with a long nose is Ek Chuah, the god of merchants.

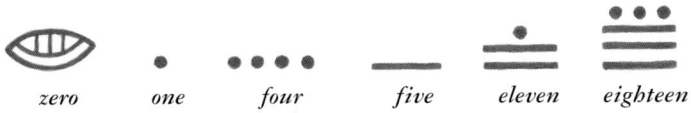

Mayan Numbers

The Mayan number system used only three signs—a dot for one, a bar for five, and the shell-symbol for zero. Other numbers were made by using a combination of those signs. When writing down large numbers, Mayan scribes put the different symbols on top of one another, rather than side by side as we do today.

4 Trace or copy Aztec or Mayan codex drawings from this book. Alternatively, make up your own, based on Mesoamerican examples.

5 Paint your tracings or drawings, using light, bright colors. Using the Mayan numbers on this page as a guide, add some numbers to your codex.

If you went to school in Aztec or Mayan times, you would find out how to recognize hundreds of different picture-symbols. You would also be taught to link them together in your mind, like a series of clues, to find out what they meant.

Time, Sun, and Stars

LIKE ALL OTHER Mesoamericans, the Maya and the Aztecs measured time using a calendar with a year of 260 days. This was used in Mexico as early as 500 BCE and is probably based on human biology—260 days is about how long it takes a baby to develop before it is born. The calendar was divided into 13 cycles of 20 days each. Mesoamerican farmers used a different calendar, based on the movements of the sun, because sunlight and the seasons made their crops grow. This calendar had 360 days, divided into 18 months of 20 days, plus five extra days that were unlucky. Every 52 years, measured in our time, these two calendars ended on the same day. For five days before the end of the 52 years, people were anxious, because they feared the world might end. A third calendar, of 584 days, also existed for calculating festival days.

SUN STONE
This massive carving was made to display the Aztec view of creation. The Aztecs believed that the world had already been created and destroyed four times and that their Fifth World was also doomed.

STUDYING THE STARS
The Caracol was constructed as an observatory to study the sky. From there, Mayan astronomers could observe the planet Venus, which was important in the Mesoamericans' measurement of time.

MAKE A SUN STONE

You will need: scissors, thick cardboard, self-drying clay, modeling tool, board, rolling pin, masking tape, white glue, glue brush, water bowl, pencil, thin cardboard, water-based paints, paintbrush, water container.

1 Cut a circle about 10 in. in diameter from thick cardboard. Roll out the clay and cut out a matching circle. Place the clay circle on the cardboard one.

2 With a modeling tool, mark a small circle in the center of the clay circle. Use a roll of masking tape as a guide. Do not cut through the clay.

3 Carve the sun god's eyes, mouth, teeth and earrings. You can use the real Aztec sun stone, shown at the top left of this page, as a guide.

alligator

wind

house

lizard

serpent

death's head

deer

rabbit

Water

dog

monkey

grass

reed

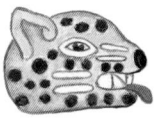

jaguar

eagle

vulture

motion

flint knife

rain

flower

Names of Days

These pictures from an Aztec codex show the 20 names for days from the farmers' calendar. These symbols were combined with a number from one to 13 to give the date, such as Three Vulture. The days were named after familiar creatures or everyday things, such as the lizard or water. Each day also had its own god. Children were often named after the day on which they were born, a custom that still continues in some parts of Mexico up to the present day.

Your finished sun stone will not be as big as the original Aztec one. That measures 13 feet across and is the largest Aztec sculpture discovered so far.

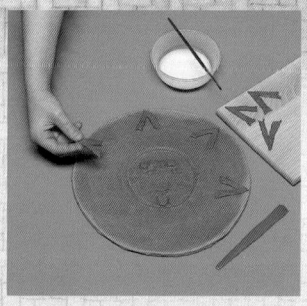

4 Roll out more clay and cut out some sun's rays, a tongue and eyebrows. Glue them to the clay circle. Smooth the edges with water and let dry.

5 Copy the 20 Aztec symbols (*above*) for days onto squares of thin cardboard. The cardboard squares should be no more than ¾ in. x ¾ in. Cut out. Paint brown.

6 Cover the clay circle with a thin coat of dark brown paint. Let it dry. Then add a thin coat of white paint to make the circle look like stone.

7 Glue the cardboard symbols evenly around the edge of the clay circle, as shown. Paint the sun stone with a thin layer of white glue to seal and varnish it.

Gods and Goddesses

RELIGION WAS a powerful force throughout Mesoamerica. It affected everything people did, from getting up in the morning to digging in their fields or obeying their ruler's laws. Everyone believed that the gods governed human life. People could not fight their decisions, but the gods could sometimes be persuaded to grant favors if they were offered gifts and sacrifices. The Aztecs and Maya believed in ancient nature gods such as the fire god, the god of corn, and the god of rain, and worshipped them with splendid festivals and ceremonies. Mesoamerican people also honored the spirits of their dead rulers. The Aztecs had their own special tribal god, Huitzilopochtli, Lord of the Sun. He rewarded his followers with victories in war.

Religious ceremonies and sacrifices were led by temple priests. With long, matted hair, red-rimmed eyes, and painted bodies splattered with blood, they were a terrifying sight.

GOD OF SPRING
Xipe Totec was the Aztec god of fertility. He protected the young shoots of corn. Each year, captives were skinned alive as a sacrifice to him. Priests dressed in their skins in religious ceremonies to remind everyone of the skin of young plants.

CHACMOOL FIGURE
This stone statue from the city of Chichen-Itza shows a Chacmool, or reclining figure. It is holding a stone slab on which offerings may have been made.

A STATUE OF A GOD

You will need: pencil, paper, self-drying clay, modeling tool, water bowl, petroleum jelly, cotton balls, plaster of Paris, terra-cotta paint, small paintbrush.

1 Make a drawing of any Aztec god. Model it as a flat figure from self-drying clay. Keep it flat on the bottom. Let the clay figure dry.

2 Completely cover the surface of your model with petroleum jelly. Then smooth a layer of clay over the jelly, pressing it down gently into any grooves.

3 Spread more clay on top to make a strong rectangular block, at least 1 in. thick. This will become your mold. Let it dry thoroughly.

Sun and Jaguar

This Mayan carving was part of a wall at Campeche in southeastern Mexico. It shows the sun god, whom the Maya called Kinich Ahau. The Maya believed that he disappeared into the underworld every night, at sunset. It was there that he turned into a fierce jaguar god. At the beginning of every new day, they believed that Kinich Ahau then returned to earth as the life-giving sun.

Water and Rain

Tlaloc was the Aztec god of life-giving rain, "the god who makes things grow." Under different names, he was worshipped throughout Mesoamerica. Tlaloc was honored when he sent water to nourish the crops and feared when he sent deadly floods. In times of drought, the Aztecs sacrificed babies to Tlaloc. They believed the babies' tears would make rain fall.

Earth Mother

This huge statue of Coatlicue (Great Lady Serpent Skirt) stood in the Sacred Precinct at Tenochtitlan. She was the fearsome Aztec earthmother goddess. Coatlicue gave birth to the Aztecs' national god, Huitzilopochtli, the moon goddess, and the stars.

This model (right) *is based on an Aztec statue. It shows a goddess holding two children. Figures of gods were often created from molds* (left).

4 Carefully ease the little model out of the solid block, using the modeling tool. The petroleum jelly should ensure that it comes out cleanly.

5 Clean any loose bits of clay from the mold and smear petroleum jelly inside. Use a cotton ball to make sure the jelly is pushed into every part.

6 Mix up some plaster of Paris and pour it into the mold. Tap the mold gently to remove any air bubbles. Let the plaster dry for at least an hour.

7 Gently remove the plaster statue from the mold. Dust it with a brush, then paint it a terra-cotta color, so that it looks like an Aztec pottery figure.

Temples and Sacrifices

MESOAMERICAN PEOPLE believed that unless they made offerings of blood and human lives to the gods, the sun would die and the world would come to an end. Mayan rulers pricked themselves with cactus thorns and stingray spines, or drew spiked cords through their tongues, to draw blood. They pulled out captives' fingernails so the blood flowed or threw them into holy water-holes. Aztecs pricked their earlobes each morning and collected two drops of blood to give to the gods. They also went to war to capture prisoners. On special occasions, vast numbers of captives were needed for sacrifice. It was reported that 20,000 victims were sacrificed to celebrate the completion of the Great Temple at Tenochtitlan in 1487. It took four days to kill them all. Mesoamerican temples were tombs as well as places of sacrifice. Rulers and their wives were buried inside. Each ruler aimed to build a great temple as a memorial to his reign.

TEMPLE TOMB
Pyramid Temple 1 at Tikal was built in the 700s CE as a memorial to a Mayan king. Nine stone platforms were built above the burial chamber to create a tall pyramid shape reaching up to the sky.

HOLY KNIFE
This sacrificial knife has a blade made from a semiprecious stone called chalcedony. It was made by Mixtecs from south Mexico. Mesoamerican priests used finely decorated knives of flint, obsidian, and other hard stones to kill captives for sacrifice. These were trimmed to be as sharp as glass.

A PYRAMID TEMPLE

You will need: pencil, ruler, thick cardboard, scissors, white glue, glue brush, masking tape, thin strips of balsa wood, thin card, corrugated cardboard, water bowl, paintbrushes, paints.

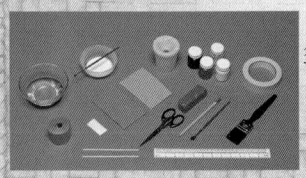

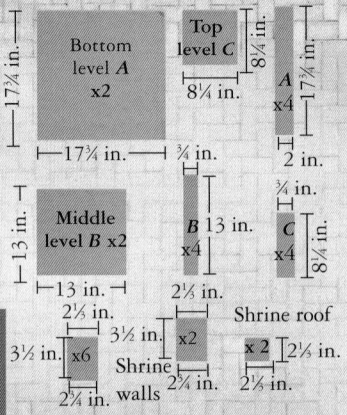

Cut out pieces for the pyramid and temple-top shrines from thick card, as shown above.

1 Use white glue and masking tape to join the thick cardboard pieces to make three flat boxes (A, B, and C). Leave the boxes until the glue is completely dry.

2 From the remaining pieces of cardboard, make the two temple-top shrines, as shown. You could add extra details with strips of balsa wood or thin cardboard.

SKULL SHRINE
Rows of human skulls, carved in stone, decorate this shrine outside the Aztecs' Great Temple in the center of Tenochtitlan. Most Aztec temples also had skull racks, where rows of real human heads were displayed. They were cut from the bodies of sacrificed captives.

HUMAN SACRIFICE
This Aztec codex painting shows captives being sacrificed. At the top, you can see a priest cutting open a captive's chest and removing the heart as an offering to the gods.

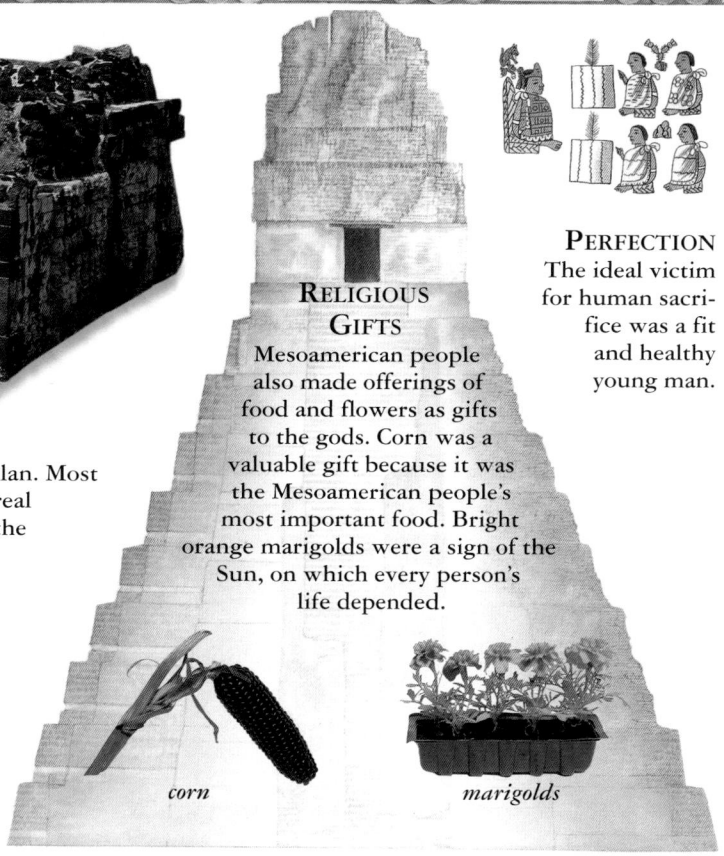

RELIGIOUS GIFTS
Mesoamerican people also made offerings of food and flowers as gifts to the gods. Corn was a valuable gift because it was the Mesoamerican people's most important food. Bright orange marigolds were a sign of the Sun, on which every person's life depended.

PERFECTION
The ideal victim for human sacrifice was a fit and healthy young man.

This model is based on the Great Temple that stood in the center of Tenochtitlan.

3 Glue the boxes, one on top of the next. Cut out pieces of cardboard the same size as each side of your boxes. They should be about ¾ in. wide. Stick down, as shown.

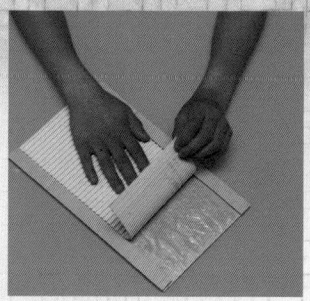

4 Cut out two strips of cardboard ¾ in. x 10¼ in. Glue them to a third piece of cardboard 5½ in. x 10¼ in. Glue corrugated cardboard 3¾ in. x 10¼ in. in position.

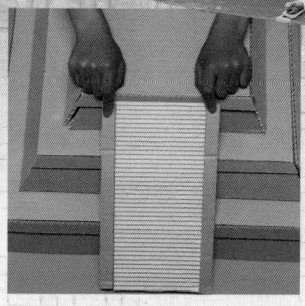

5 Stick the staircase to the front of the temple, as shown. Use a ruler to check that the staircase is an equal distance from either side of the temple.

6 Paint the whole temple a cream color to look like natural stone. Add details, such as carvings or wall paintings, using brightly colored paint.

Time for Celebration

FESTIVALS, WITH MUSIC AND DANCING, were a very important part of Mesoamerican life. All big Aztec and Mayan cities had a huge open space in the center, where crowds gathered to sing and dance to honor the gods on festival days. Every twenty days, there were celebrations to mark the start of a new month. There were also festivals, with prayers and sacrifices, to mark important seasons of the farming year. In July and August, the Aztecs celebrated flowering trees and plants. In September, there were harvest festivals, and in October, festivals where hunters gave thanks for plentiful prey. For the Aztec rulers and their guests, feasts and entertainment were a regular event.

All of these special occasions involved music and song. Favorite instruments included rattles, whistles, ocarinas, flutes, bells, and shells blown like trumpets. Aztec musicians also played a two-tone wooden drum, called a *teponaztli*, to provide a lively beat for dancing. Stringed instruments were unknown until after the Spanish conquest.

FESTIVAL BEAT
This Mayan priest is shown in a wall painting in the royal palace at the city of Bonampak. He is taking part in a procession to the temple, celebrating the birth of a royal child.

AN AZTEC ORCHESTRA
Musicians played conch shells, rattles, and drums while crowds of worshippers sang and danced in the main square of Tenochtitlan.

AN AZTEC RATTLE

You will need: self-drying clay, modeling tool, plastic wrap, water bowl, dried melon seeds, bamboo cane, white and terra-cotta paint, paintbrush, water container, feather, white glue, glue brush.

1 Make a solid model gourd from self-drying clay. You can copy the shape shown above. When it is dry, wrap the "gourd" completely in plastic wrap.

2 Cover the wrapped model gourd with an outer layer of self-drying clay about ¾ in. thick. Smooth the clay with water to give an even surface.

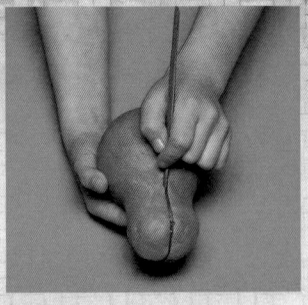

3 Let the outer layer of clay get hard but not completely solid. Cut it in half with the thin end of the modeling tool and remove the model gourd.

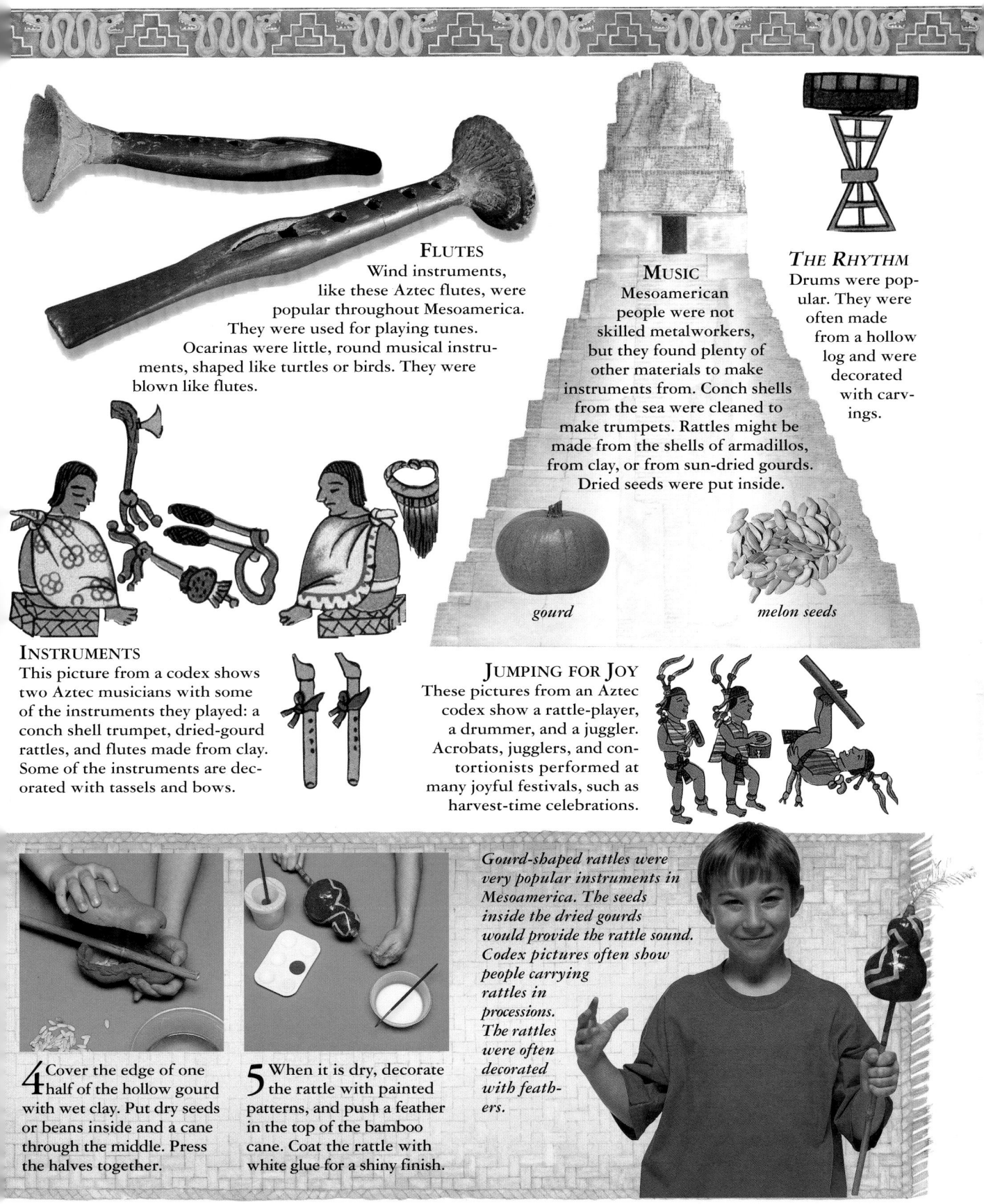

FLUTES
Wind instruments, like these Aztec flutes, were popular throughout Mesoamerica. They were used for playing tunes. Ocarinas were little, round musical instruments, shaped like turtles or birds. They were blown like flutes.

MUSIC
Mesoamerican people were not skilled metalworkers, but they found plenty of other materials to make instruments from. Conch shells from the sea were cleaned to make trumpets. Rattles might be made from the shells of armadillos, from clay, or from sun-dried gourds. Dried seeds were put inside.

gourd

melon seeds

THE RHYTHM
Drums were popular. They were often made from a hollow log and were decorated with carvings.

INSTRUMENTS
This picture from a codex shows two Aztec musicians with some of the instruments they played: a conch shell trumpet, dried-gourd rattles, and flutes made from clay. Some of the instruments are decorated with tassels and bows.

JUMPING FOR JOY
These pictures from an Aztec codex show a rattle-player, a drummer, and a juggler. Acrobats, jugglers, and contortionists performed at many joyful festivals, such as harvest-time celebrations.

4 Cover the edge of one half of the hollow gourd with wet clay. Put dry seeds or beans inside and a cane through the middle. Press the halves together.

5 When it is dry, decorate the rattle with painted patterns, and push a feather in the top of the bamboo cane. Coat the rattle with white glue for a shiny finish.

Gourd-shaped rattles were very popular instruments in Mesoamerica. The seeds inside the dried gourds would provide the rattle sound. Codex pictures often show people carrying rattles in processions. The rattles were often decorated with feathers.

Sports and Games

MESOAMERICAN PEOPLE enjoyed sports and games after work and on festival days. Two favorite games were *tlachtli* or *ulama*, the famous Mesoamerican ball game, and *patolli*, a board game. The ball game was played in front of huge crowds, while *patolli* was a quieter game. Mesoamerican games were not just for fun. Both the ball game and *patolli* had religious meanings. In the first, the court symbolized the world, and the rubber ball stood for the sun as it made its daily journey across the sky. Players were meant to keep the ball moving in order to give energy to the sun. Losing teams were sometimes sacrificed as offerings to the sun god. In *patolli*, the movement of markers on the board represented the passing years.

PATOLLI
A group of Aztecs are shown here playing the game of *patolli*. It was played by moving dried beans or clay counters along a cross-shaped board with 52 squares. It could be very exciting. Players often bet on the results.

THE ACROBAT
This Olmec statue shows a very supple acrobat. Mesoamericans admired youth, fitness, and beauty. Sports were fun, but they could also be good training for the demands of war. Being fit was considered attractive.

FLYING MEN
Volador was a ceremony performed on religious festival days. Four men, dressed as birds and attached to ropes, jumped off a high pole. As they spun around, falling toward the ground, they circled the pole 13 times each. That made 52 circuits—the length of the Mesoamerican holy calendar cycle.

PLAY PATOLLI

***You will need:** thick cardboard, pencil, ruler, black felt tip pen, paints, small paintbrush, water container, colored papers, scissors, dried beans, self-drying clay, white glue, and glue brush.*

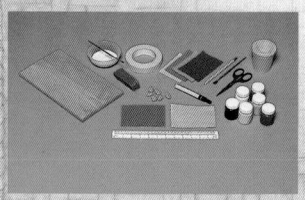

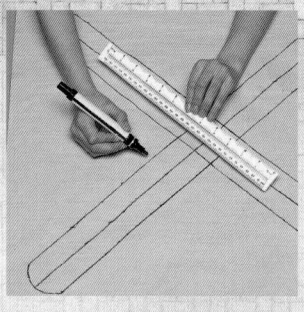

1 Measure a square of thick cardboard about 20 in. x 20 in. Using a felt tip pen and a ruler, draw three lines from corner to corner to make a cross shape.

2 Draw seven pairs of spaces along each arm. The third space in from the end should be a double space. Paint triangles in it.

3 Draw eight jaguar heads and eight marigold flowers on different colored paper. Cut them out. Paint the face of the sun god in the center.

Target Ring

This stone ring comes from Chichen-Itza. Ball game players used only their hips and knees to hit a solid rubber ball through rings like this fixed high on the ball-court walls.

All Dressed Up

A man dressed to play in a Mesoamerican ball game is shown in this terra-cotta statue. The figure was made around 800 CE on the Mayan island of Jaina, off the western coast of the Yucatan Peninsula. He wears a protective belt of leather and wood, padded wrist guards and knee guards, a pointed cap, and big earrings. Being a ball game player was risky but could bring rich rewards. Winners were sometimes allowed to claim the spectators' clothes and jewels as prizes.

Play Ball

The ruins of a huge ball court can still be seen in the Mayan city of Uxmal. The biggest courts were up to 65½ yards long and were built next to temples, in the centers of cities. People crowded inside the court to watch. Play was fast, furious, and dangerous. Many players were injured as they clashed with opponents.

4 Stick the jaguars and marigolds randomly on the board. Paint a blue circle at the end of one arm, and a crown at the opposite end. Repeat in green.

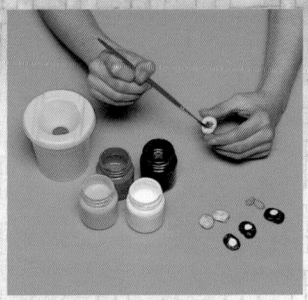

5 Paint five dried beans black with a white dot in the middle of one side. The beans will be thrown as dice. Make two markers. Paint one green and one blue.

Most of the original rules for patolli have been lost. In this version, start each marker on the circle of the same color. The goal is to move your marker to the crown of the same color and back. You lose a turn if you land on a jaguar and get an extra turn if you land on a marigold.

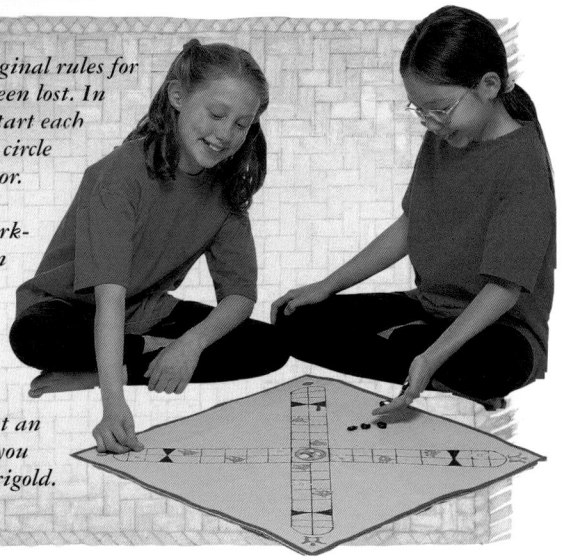

Myths, Legends, and Omens

THE AZTECS lived in constant fear that their world might come to an end. Ancient legends told that this had happened four times before. Each time, the world had been born again. Yet Aztec priests and astrologers did not believe that this would happen the next time. If the world ended a fifth time, it would be forever. The souls of all Aztec people would be banished to a dark, gloomy underworld. The Wind of Knives would cut the flesh from their bones, and living skeletons would feast and dance with the Lord of the Dead. Then the Aztecs would vanish forever when they reached Mictlan (hell).

The Maya told similar stories about the underworld—which they called Xibalba (the Place of Fright) in a great epic poem, the *Popol Vuh*. This poem featured two brothers called the Hero Twins.

Aztec legends also told that the end of the world would be heralded by strange signs. In 1519 CE these gloomy prophecies seemed to be coming true. Ruler Moctezuma II had weird, worrisome dreams. Astronomers also observed eclipses of the sun and a moving comet with a fiery tail.

FEATHERED SERPENT
Quetzalcoatl was an ancient god-king. His name meant feathered-serpent. He was worshipped by many Mesoamerican people, but especially by the Toltecs. They believed that he had sacrificed himself to help his people. A Toltec legend said that one day he would return, heralding the end of the world.

HEROES AND LEGENDS
This court is in Copan, Guatemala. The ball game featured in many Mayan legends about the Hero Twins. They were skilled ball game players and also expert hunters with deadly blow guns.

Creatures of Legend

This Mayan bowl is decorated with a picture of a spider monkey. Many different kinds of monkeys lived in the rainforests of Mesoamerica. Monkey-gods played an important part in Mayan myths and legends. Because monkeys were quick and clever, the Maya believed that monkey-gods protected clever people, like scribes.

The New Fire Ceremony

Every 52 years, the Aztecs believed that the world might come to an end. To stop this from happening, they held a special ceremony. People put out their fires and stayed indoors. At sunset, priests climbed to the top of a hill and waited for the planet Venus to appear in the sky. At the moment it appeared, a captive was sacrificed to the gods. His heart was ripped out and a fire lit in his chest. The priests then sent messengers all over the Aztec lands, carrying torches to relight the fires. People then believed the world was safe for another 52 years.

Heavenly Messenger

The ruler Moctezuma is shown here observing the brilliant comet that appeared in the Mexican sky in 1519. Aztec people carefully studied the stars for messages from the gods. They remembered the old Toltec legend that said that one day the god Quetzalcoatl would return and bring the world to an end.

Aztec Heritage

Many Aztec and Mayan traditions still survive today. Millions of people speak Nahuatl (the Aztecs' language) or Mayan languages.

Aztec and Mayan beliefs have mingled with Christian traditions to create new religious festivals. The most famous of these festivals is the Day of the Dead. Families bring presents of flowers and candies shaped like skulls to their ancestors' graves.

Against the Aztecs
This picture comes from *The History of the Indies*. It was written by Diego Duran, a Spanish friar who had sympathy for the Aztecs. Spanish soldiers and their allies from Tlaxcalla are seen fighting against the Aztecs. Although the Aztecs fought bravely, they had no chance of defeating Spanish soldiers mounted on horseback and armed with guns.

The Coming of the Spanish

In 1493, the explorer Christopher Columbus arrived back in Spain from his pioneering voyage across the Atlantic Ocean. He told tales of an extraordinary "new world" full of gold. Excited by Columbus's stories, a group of Spanish soldiers sailed to Mexico in 1519, hoping to make their fortunes. They were led by a nobleman called Hernan Cortes. Together with the Aztecs' enemies, he led a march on Tenochtitlan. For the next two years, the Aztecs fought to stop Cortes and his soldiers from taking over their land. At first, they had some success, driving the Spaniards out of Tenochtitlan in May, 1520. Then, in 1521, Cortes attacked the city again, set fire to its buildings, and killed around three-quarters of the population. In 1535, Mexico became a colony, ruled by officials sent from Spain.

A similar thing happened in Mayan lands, but more slowly. The Spanish first landed there in 1523. They did not conquer the last independent city-state, Tayasal, until 1697.

A Sad Night
On May 6, 1520, Spanish soldiers massacred Aztecs gathered for a religious festival in Tenochtitlan. The citizens were outraged and attacked the Spaniards, many of whom died. During this night, the emperor Moctezuma II was stoned to death, probably by Aztecs who believed he had betrayed them. Cortes called this the *Noche Triste* (sad night).

The End of Aztec Power
This Aztec picture shows the surrender of Cuauhtemoc, the last Aztec king, to Cortes. After Moctezuma II died in 1520, the Aztecs were led by two of Moctezuma's descendants—Cuitlahuac, who ruled for only one year, and Cuauhtemoc. He was the last king and reigned until 1524.

Running for Their Lives

This illustration from a Spanish manuscript shows Aztec people fleeing from Spanish conquerors. You can see heavily burdened porters carrying stocks of food and household goods across a river to safety. On the far bank, mothers and children, with a pet bird and dog, hide behind huge maguey cactus plants.

Working Like Slaves

Spanish settlers in Mexico took over all the Aztec and Mayan fields and forced the people to work as farm laborers. They treated them cruelly, almost like slaves. This modern picture shows a Spanish overseer giving orders.

After the Conquest

Mexican artist Diego Rivera shows Mesoamerica after the Spanish conquest. Throughout the 1500s and 1600s, settlers from Spain arrived there. They drove out the local nobles and forced ordinary people to work for them. Spanish missionaries tried to replace local beliefs with European customs and Christianity. In Tenochtitlan, the Spaniards pulled down splendid Aztec palaces and temples to build churches and fine homes for themselves. You can see gangs of Aztec men working as laborers in the background of this picture.

Glossary

adobe Sun-dried mud bricks, used as a building material.

ahaw One of the special names the Maya gave to their rulers.

amaranth A bushy plant with edible seeds.

ancestors Those from whom a person descended.

ball court The place where the Mesoamerican ball game was played. A large, open courtyard surrounded by rows of stone seats.

barter Exchanging goods for others of equal value.

chinampa An Aztec garden built on the fertile, reclaimed land on the lake shore.

clan A group of people related to one another through their ancestors or by marriage.

cochineal A red dye made from crushed beetles.

codex A folding book.

compost Rotting vegetation used to make the soil fertile.

conch shell The huge horn-shaped shell of a tropical sea creature. It was used as a musical instrument in Mesoamerican lands.

dugout canoe A type of canoe made by hollowing out a tree trunk.

garrison A band of soldiers living in a particular place.

glyph A picture-symbol used in the Mesoamerican system of writing.

herbalism Trying to heal people with medicines made of herbs.

human sacrifice Killing humans as an offering to the gods.

jade A smooth, green stone. Jade was highly prized in Mesoamerica.

katun A Mayan measurement of time—72,000 days.

litter A portable bed on which Mesoamerican rulers were carried. loom A piece of equipment used to weave cloth.

macehualtin The Aztec name for ordinary people.

mahk'ina One of the special names the Maya gave to their rulers.

mosaic Tiny pieces of stone, shell, or glass used to decorate objects.

obsidian A black, glassy stone. It is produced when volcanoes erupt.

patolli A popular Aztec board game.

peninsula An area of land surrounded by sea on three sides, making it almost like an island.

plaza A big open space in the center of a town or city.

pulque An Aztec fermented drink.

silt Fine grains of soil found at the bottom of rivers and lakes.

slash and burn A method of farming in the rainforest.

stucco Plaster used to cover and decorate important stone buildings, such as temples.

tamales Dumplings made of corn with a meat or vegetable filling.

tlachtli Aztec name for the ballgame played throughout Mesoamerica.

tortillas Corn pancakes.

tribute Taxes paid in goods by conquered people.

uictli A Mesoamerican digging stick used like a spade.

yucca A desert plant with long, fleshy leaves.

For More Information

Mundo Maya Organisation
World Heritage PACT
World Heritage Centre
7, place de Fontenoy
75007 Paris, France
Web site: http://whc.unesco.org/en/partners/35
An organization of countries in South and Central America, united to preserve the history of the Mayan people.

National Museum of Anthropology
Chapultepec Polanco
Mexico City, Mexico
Web site: http://www.mna.inah.gob.mx/
A national museum that houses many pieces of Mayan and Aztec history.

Web Sites

Due to the changing nature of Internet links, Rosen Publishing has developed an online list of Web sites related to the subject of this book. This site is updated regularly. Please use this link to access the list:

http://www.rosenlinks.com/pttp/azma

For Further Reading

Aguilar-Moreno, Manuel. *Handbook to Life in the Aztec World*. New York, NY: Oxford University Press, 2007.

Coe, Michael D. *The Maya*, Seventh Edition. London, England: Thames & Hudson, 2005.

Phillips, Charles. *The Art & Architecture of the Aztec & Maya*. London, England: Southwater, 2008.

Smith, Michael E. *Aztec City-State Capitals*. Gainesville, FL: University Press of Florida, 2008.

Sonneborn, Liz. *The Ancient Aztecs*. London, England: Franklin Watts, 2005.

Townsend, Richard F. *The Aztecs*. London, England: Thames & Hudson, 2000.

Webster, David L. *The Fall of the Ancient Maya: Solving the Mystery of the Maya Collapse*. London, England: Thames & Hudson, 2002.

Index

A

alcohol 18, 28
astronomy 9, 10, 14, 48, 58–9

B

ball game 56–7, 58
barter 37
blood offerings 41, 52
boats 38, 39
Bonampak 5, 32
buildings 5, 8, 12, 13, 20–1, 46
burial 5, 8, 10, 20, 34, 43, 52

C

cactus plants 13, 18, 28, 30, 31, 32, 52
calendars 6, 48–9, 56, 59
canals 22, 39
Caracol 48
Chacmool 50
Chichen-Itza 5, 6, 7, 42, 50, 57
Chichimec 7
children 14–17, 32
chile peppers 14, 16, 28, 31, 45
chinampas 7, 24–5, 39
city-states 42–3
Classic era 4, 6
clothes 10, 11, 16–17, 18, 32–3, 34, 35, 40–1
cochineal beetles 17, 26
cocoa 25, 27, 29, 37
codex books 4, 5, 46–7
Columbus, Christopher 9, 60
Copan 5, 7, 12, 18, 20, 24, 43, 46, 58
corn 11, 15, 16, 19, 24, 28–9, 36, 50, 53
Cortes, Hernan 9, 60
craftworkers 34–5, 36

D

dogs 29, 38–9, 61
dyes 17, 26, 27

E

education 14, 46–7

F

family life 14–17
fans 12–13, 19, 34
farming 4, 7, 11, 19, 24–5, 28, 36, 48, 50, 51, 54
feathers 12–13, 19, 26, 27, 33, 34, 37, 40, 41
festivals 48, 54–5, 56
fire ceremony 59
fishing 26–7, 28
food 11, 14, 15, 16, 18, 19, 24–9, 36, 37, 53
furs 26, 27, 37, 40, 41

G

games 56–7
glyphs 43, 46–7
gods and goddesses 50–3, 54, 58–9
gold 6, 32–3, 35, 40

H

hairstyles 33, 40, 50
houses 20–1, 30
Huastec 33
Huitzilopochtli 22, 23, 50, 51
hunting 19, 26–7, 28

I

irrigation 4

J

jade 4, 35, 37, 43
jewelry 32–3, 34–5, 42, 45

K

Kabah 5, 8
Kinich Ahau 51

L

laws 10, 12–13, 14, 25, 36
lip-plugs 32

M

Malintzin 9
markets 36–7, 39
masks 4, 5, 7, 15, 34–5, 43
medicine 14, 26, 30–1
merchants 36–7, 47

Mesoamerica 4–7
metalwork 6, 32-3, 35
Mixtec 6, 7, 32, 52
Moctezuma II 9, 12, 58, 59, 60
Monte Alban 7
mosaics 34–5
music 54–5

N

numbers 46–7

O

obsidian 15, 35, 41, 52
Ocelotl 41
Olmec 4, 6, 56

P

Pacal, Lord 5, 8, 43
palaces 12–13, 18
Palenque 5, 6, 7, 8, 43
paper 37, 46
patolli 56–7
pilgrims 42
Popol Vuh 58
Postclassic era 6
pottery 4, 10, 16, 27, 28, 34–5, 36–7, 42, 46
Preclassic era 4, 6
priests 50, 52–3, 54
punishment 13, 14
Putun 5, 6, 42

Q

Quetzalcoatl 6, 58, 59

R

religion 5, 6, 9, 10–13, 14, 18, 22–3, 24, 30, 42, 50–5
Rivera, Diego 24, 30, 35, 61

S

sacrifice 6, 9, 22-3, 40, 41, 42, 44–5, 50–3, 54, 56, 59
scribes 10, 44, 46–7
skull racks 53
slash and burn 24, 25
Spaniards 4, 9, 23, 34, 38, 41, 47, 60–1
steam baths 31
stelae 12, 43
sun stone 48–9

T

Tenochtitlan 7, 8, 9, 21, 22–3, 24, 35, 40, 44, 45, 51, 52, 53, 60
Teotihuacan 4, 5, 6, 7, 18
Texcoco, Lake 7, 22–3, 24–5, 39
Tikal 5, 7, 18, 35, 42
Toltec 4, 6, 7, 40, 58
trade 6, 8, 27, 35, 36–7, 39, 40, 42
tribute 8, 11, 14, 16, 25, 27, 35, 36, 40, 44, 45
Triple Alliance 8, 44
Tula 6, 7, 40
turquoise 7, 34, 35, 45

W

warriors 10, 11, 22, 30, 33, 35, 40–1, 44–5, 52, 56
water supply 22, 43, 51
weaving 7, 16–17
women 10–11, 12, 14–17, 28–9, 30, 32–3, 36, 37, 46
writing 4, 5, 8, 10, 11, 14, 43, 46–7, 49

Z

Zapotec 4

About the Author

Fiona Macdonald is a highly experienced children's author, specializing in history. She has written or contributed to a number of books, including one on the art of keeping clean, which won *The Times Educational Supplement's* Senior Information Book Award.